PRAISE FOR *GIVING BACK*

We all lead busy lives: raising children, developing careers, managing households, making payments—most days we are like circus entertainers spinning eight plates on six sticks. No matter your age or stage in life, put the sticks down and let the plates tumble to the ground. Take 20 minutes each morning for a week, and read Giving Back. Author Linda Marshall will gently and thoughtfully remind you of the importance of families, expressing gratitude, and leading from where you are. We have learned much from those who raised us, and we can share those attributes with our families whether those families are composed of blood relatives or valued friends. Marshall, through a series of engaging questions, rekindles an often forgotten habit of expressing gratitude. Fortunate to live in a first world country, we have so very little to whine about. Finally, there is an entire chapter devoted to personal leadership skills. Marshall chooses classic quotes on leadership from well-known authors to illustrate the importance and strengths of servant leadership. It's not about becoming the chief-whatever or the executive manager or the super boss; it's about leading from where you are to accomplish personal, workplace, and community goals. After reading Giving Back, you might be tempted to lead a more joyful life, free of stressful juggling acts and focused on strengthening strong and positive relationships with family, friends, work-colleagues, and community members.

—Valerie Parke, Professor and Librarian
Language Studies Department, *Mohawk College*

T0145799

Linda is an exceptional example of a woman who is dedicated to the growth and vitality of her community through voluntary service. Her professional demeanor, creativity, and positivity are the hallmarks of a true communicator and community leader.

—Carol Kehoe, Executive Director
HPO Hamilton Philharmonic Orchestra

Not only does Linda Marshall have a passion for giving back, in her personal life she has taken this passion into action. This book's unique perspective is supported by the fact (and the old adage). Been there, done that.

—Jim Baske, CEO
ArcelorMittal North America

Linda is a role model philanthropist, leading by example and demonstrating generosity in everything she does. Linda donates at significant levels and readily goes out of her way, even on a moment's notice, to help our United Way. We're grateful for Linda's eagerness to lend her name and a hand for raising awareness of the needs in our community.

—Jeff Vallentin, CEO
United Way Burlington & Greater Hamilton

Linda is an excellent community role model, and her tireless commitment and compassion to community is inspiring.

—Lou Celli, CPA, CA, Partner
Privately Held Business Leader–Southern Ontario
Grant Thornton LLP

Like the author herself, this book exudes positivity. It will have you reviewing your own experiences and attitudes to improve your enjoyment of life.

—Karen Pashleigh, Chief Human Resources Officer
Mohawk College

Linda is not only a woman of distinction; she is an incredible human being and example to us all.

—Daniel Banko, CEO
BANKOMEDIA

I loved reading Giving Back. *Linda Marshall provides a powerful dose of inspiration combined with compelling questions for you to consider for enrichment of your life and others. This will be my go-to guide for many years to come. Give a copy to your loved ones!*

—Kelly Ann Pauly, World Class Continuous
Improvement Manager, *ArcelorMittal Dofasco*

Linda possesses a unique ability to capture the commitment and dedication of people through enthusiasm and belief in a cause.

—Rob MacIsaac, President and CEO
Hamilton Health Sciences

Linda is an individual who exudes amazing energy and is extremely driven to help support her community. Her most valuable asset is her attitude, which is one of optimism with a determined focus on getting the task completed regardless of the obstacles.

—Carmela Trombetta, Vice President Commercial Markets
RBC Royal Bank Hamilton Commercial Financial Services

Linda has a calming effect as a leader and is so universally loved and respected that her ability to connect people and organizations can seem effortless.

—Marc Ayotte, Head of College
Hillfield Strathallan College

A refreshing account outlining the extraordinary effects of giving back while finding purpose and clarity in today's fast paced environment. I especially enjoyed the recommendations offered in the "consider this" sections.

—Dr. Steve Szarka B. Eng., M. Eng., MD., CFPC, FCFP
Assistant Clinical Professor, *McMaster University*

I have had the opportunity to work with and meet many great, influential community leaders and philanthropists. Linda Marshall truly stands out above many of them.

—Karen Shea, Crown Counsel
Ministry of the Attorney General

In the chaotic pace of today's world, who would ever consider "giving back," or associate this notion with living life fully? Linda Marshall makes the connection obvious in her book. She is an exceptional woman who believes deeply in people's capacity to live life fully through giving. It provides a wonderful and inspiring approach to each day. Thank you, Linda.

—Gregg Crealock, Team Leader, Professional Services Division
BMW Canada Sales Master, *Budds' BMW*

Linda is an outstanding community leader, giving of her time to ensure others benefit.

—Glenn Harkness, Executive Director
Boys and Girls Clubs of Hamilton

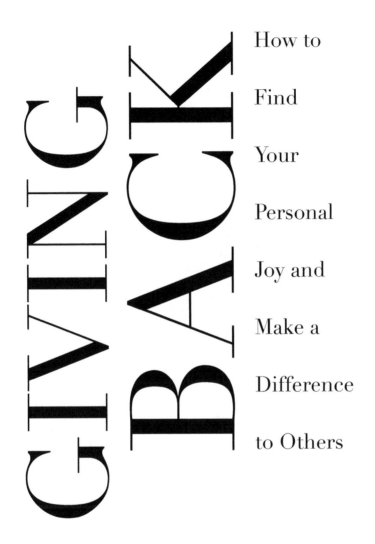

GIVING BACK

How to Find Your Personal Joy and Make a Difference to Others

GIVING BACK

How to Find Your Personal Joy and Make a Difference to Others

LINDA MARSHALL

Published by Advantage, Charleston, South Carolina.
Member of Advantage Media Group.

ADVANTAGE is a registered trademark and the Advantage colophon is a trademark of Advantage Media Group, Inc.

Printed in the United States of America.

ISBN: 978-1-59932-597-2
LCCN: 2015946641

This publication is designed to provide accurate and authoritative information in regard to the subject matter covered. It is sold with the understanding that the publisher is not engaged in rendering legal, accounting, or other professional services. If legal advice or other expert assistance is required, the services of a competent professional person should be sought.

Advantage Media Group is proud to be a part of the Tree Neutral® program. Tree Neutral offsets the number of trees consumed in the production and printing of this book by taking proactive steps such as planting trees in direct proportion to the number of trees used to print books. To learn more about Tree Neutral, please visit www.treeneutral.com. To learn more about Advantage's commitment to being a responsible steward of the environment, please visit www.advantagefamily.com/green

Advantage Media Group is a publisher of business, self-improvement, and professional development books and online learning. We help entrepreneurs, business leaders, and professionals share their Stories, Passion, and Knowledge to help others Learn & Grow. Do you have a manuscript or book idea that you would like us to consider for publishing? Please visit advantagefamily.com or call 1.866.775.1696.

For my parents, who encouraged me on my journey to excellence. They taught me how to give unconditionally, the value of working hard toward a goal, and the importance of never giving up. They continue to be the wind beneath my wings.

CONTACT LINDA:

To schedule Linda to speak at your event, consult or conduct a workshop/seminar,

email linda@marshallconnects.com

or call 289.800.1288

For more information, go to the following website:

www.marshallconnects.com

TABLE OF CONTENTS

A WORD FROM THE AUTHOR

Giving has been a huge part of my journey in life. From my earliest memories, it has shaped me as an individual and has brought me great joy. In writing this book, my hope is to share the giving moments that changed my life for the better and to encourage others to consider such opportunities.

If doing something for others can enrich one's own life, then it is truly a win-win. I strongly believe that each of us needs to return, with a grateful heart, a portion of what has been given to us. Those who have heard me speak or have attended my workshops understand my commitment to spreading that passion to others. I do so through my business, Marshall Connects.

But I must emphasize that this book is not about me. My hope is that in sharing my giving moments, it will encourage others to consider the opportunities they can provide in changing the lives of those around them. By openly sharing my heart, my laughter and tears, my joys and struggles, I hope you will relive moments in your own life—moments on your own journey.

In my speaking engagements, I help people appreciate what truly matters in their workplaces and in their personal lives. Life is short; we hold it in the palms of our hands, and we need to turn our attention to reflecting on what is most meaningful. We need to put our lives in perspective and approach each day with gratitude. When we can do that, we can experience the joy that motivates giving back.

—Linda Marshall

ABOUT THE AUTHOR

As president of Marshall Connects, Linda brings more than 30 years of experience working with and educating teams to strive for excellence and reach their potential. As a member of the Canadian Association of Professional Speakers (CAPS), she offers a wealth of workshop and consulting services and is a certified Personality Dimensions® facilitator.

Linda has developed strengths in strategy, team building, board development, and business planning, with demonstrated success in the management of complex, multisite operations. She is an expert in leveraging her strengths as a connector and collaborator and in setting and achieving goals in challenging and often fast-paced environments.

During her career at Mohawk College, Linda held 18 leadership positions in the areas of Early Childhood Education, Staff Development, Human Resources, Corporate Services, Alumni Relations, Public and Media Relations, Special Events, Special Projects in Advancement and Development, Annual and Planned Giving, Student Sponsorship, and Student Services.

Linda Marshall has been an active member of her community for over three decades. She has been a strong volunteer and civic leader with a philanthropic heart, benefiting over a dozen agencies and organizations. She works best when she is helping others, and with this book she will continue that good work for many years to come.

ACKNOWLEDGMENTS

I want to gratefully acknowledge all of the individuals who have assisted and guided me while I was writing this book. I am truly blessed with an abundance of people in my life who are always willing to reach out, support, and energize me.

First and foremost, I want to thank my husband, Rick, and daughters Lindsay and Olivia, who love me unconditionally and are always there when I need them the most. Their love and support gave me the extra strength necessary to surmount the many challenges and opportunities over the past six months while writing this book during the opening of my new business, Marshall Connects. What mattered the most is that they believed in me!

Family is important to me, so to my siblings and my extended family who are always there if I need them, my sincerest appreciation. The same sentiment is shared with my closest connections—the people I am connected to on a regular basis who help shape my life and hold me to a high standard—they are my family, too!

Many others have supported my mind, body, and spirit over the years and have gently guided me through this last year of transition. They were the wind beneath my wings that helped me soar!

To the following people who were there for me during this particular journey:

Dan Banko	Jim Baske
Ruth Catney	Lou Celli
Chelsea Crealock	Gregg Crealock

Glenn Harkness   Carol Kehoe

Rob MacIsaac   Patti Miller

Mohawk friends and colleagues

Valerie Park   Karen Pashleigh

Kelly Ann Pauly   Cynthia Pettman

Wilma Seville   Karen Shea

Dr. Steve Szarka   Carmela Trombetta

Niki Vrbanac   Brian Webster

Shendal Yalchin   Tijen Yalchin

Jeff Vallentin

You have supported me in numerous ways that are too many to mention—you have my gratitude.

PROLOGUE: *FOUNDATIONS*

Memories surround me—some joyful and others less so, but each one is an episode in my journey. It's funny how the most mundane of moments can be the ones that endure through the years. Memories are like old, crinkled photographs, pulled out and examined again and again. They highlight the lessons we learned along the way—those "aha" moments when we laughed and smiled or fretted and cried.

I have vivid memories of times with my mother when I was very young and she was doing something special just for me. I can close my eyes even now and see it—my mom is buying a beautiful long winter coat for her little girl. This day I will have something new, not hand-me-downs. We go shopping, the two of us, and I feel special as I try the coat on. That coat kept me warm for many long Canadian winters in our hometown of Hamilton, Ontario, but the memory has warmed me for decades. Here is another moment: we have just left the hospital after a difficult test and are headed to the candy store. I think of such moments, and I feel the kind of joy that squeezes the heart. It's in these memories that I understand the real gift my mother gave to me and my siblings—she gave us the spirit of giving, and in that I find great happiness.

My parents were accustomed to hard work and challenging times for more than half their lives. They had so little, and yet growing up, I don't remember hardship. It seemed we always had so much. My mom stayed home to take care of us—my brother, two sisters, and me—and that's the life we knew. My younger sister and I both had health issues, and that must have been a difficult responsibility for my mom. She reached out to her family for support, and she received it—an unconditional kind of love.

When we were young, my dad worked long hours most of the time so that my mom could be home with us, so I have fewer early memories of him. He had a powerful presence, and he never gave up. I've learned over time that I am very much like him. Dad followed a dream until he realized it, and he was very giving by nature.

I feel so fortunate to have been raised by such people. They were decent and strong—you might say they were the ordinary stock of this world's many good people. But to me they were extraordinary—and I hope, as I share this journey of life and loss and love, that you will think fondly of such souls who have touched your own life. What will your legacy be?

THE EMBRACE OF FAMILY

The lessons I learned from my family are tools I use in life daily, though I have only realized this in the past few years since my parents died. And I had a second family, as well, the one that I spent 32 years with before I retired to begin my new journey. I had more than 18 different roles during my career at Mohawk College, all of which shaped my life. It is rare today that one spends that much time in the same place and equally rare to have so many opportunities. There, too, I learned lessons in living. I consider myself blessed to have had two strong families influence my life.

When my two daughters were small, I often would take them to visit with their Nana and Papa—my parents, Anna and Gerald Marshall—at the Florida home where they would stay warm during Canada's colder months. My parents would pack up and travel down in the fall for several weeks, come back up for Christmas, and then return south after the holidays. For many years I went down with the girls during their March Break from school for visits of a week or two. This was a wonderful opportunity for them to get to know their grandparents.

So many years later, we still laugh about those times. The simple moments—spaghetti dinners, barbecues, bike rides—are the stuff of lifelong memories. They are snapshots in time that we will have forever.

In those visits, I could feel, once again, the embracing and accepting atmosphere in which I was raised. My parents had always welcomed people into their home and reached out to help. When I was a girl, I knew that any friend of mine would be fondly welcomed by my parents.

They were there for me as the years passed. I went off to college, graduated, and married. My husband, Rick, and I joined our paths in 1982, and we have shared so much of life together, including the joys and challenges of parenthood. I am forever grateful that my daughters' memories will always include those times shared with Nana and Papa.

STRUGGLING, HEALING

My parents died young; my mother was 63 when she was diagnosed with stage four cancer. She lived for three months after her diagnosis. No one is ever really prepared for such a loss, and I am not sure my siblings and I have gotten over it. We learned to manage the loss, but to this day we all struggle with it.

My father was faced with the prospect of being alone. He had been truly committed to my mother. "You know, Linda, that's all you have," he told me once. "Commitment is the one thing you have between two people. If you lose that, if in any way you break it, you have nothing left."

I have thought about those words many times over the years. I know commitment goes beyond love and marriage. It's essential to friendship. A relationship is a gift. If you don't handle it tenderly, you may lose it. It may break. I consider my friends, too, to be family, in that we share in one another's lives. They pick me up when I have fallen and help me see that things will get better—that tomorrow is another day.

Why does it take losing someone before we realize what we have? We're all at risk of that. We're at risk of squandering the little time that we've been given here. When we suffer a loss like this, we rethink so many things. We worry more about others around us, and we ponder our own mortality.

Once I realized how short life is, I knew then that I needed to do more—at work, at home, and in my community. I began to enjoy each and every opportunity. Both of my families played such an important role in helping me through those times. I could feel the depth of their caring. I began to understand how we contribute to shaping our communities, whether in the family or in the workplace. We can sow harmony, or we can sow dysfunction. A few years later, my life had joy in it again.

About five years after my mother's death, when my father was 70 years old, he was diagnosed with cancer and died about 14 months later. It was another devastating blow to the family. So many people suffer such losses or much worse, but most find the strength to go on. Life isn't the same, but we manage. How well we do determines how we live our lives, which in turn affects everyone we interact with each day.

For everyone in the family, this was a time of major change. We all faced the loss in our own ways, and it was challenging. I felt that our love was being put to the test. To this day, my siblings and I often wonder why we had to lose our parents the way we did. Although anyone can ask "why me" or "why us," death is not personal. It just can feel that way.

When you are with the ones who brought you into the world during their last moments on earth, it changes you. Nothing will ever be the same again, nor should it be. For many, the death of their parents may be one of life's most difficult losses, but it prepares them and toughens them for the many other challenges they will face.

Once again, after mourning the death of my second parent, I found ways to give back to my family and my community to fill the void—and again I felt the joy squeezing my heart.

THE GIFTS OF THE HEART

Years later, the loss of my parents is still raw in my heart. I feel the pangs of sadness most poignantly at Christmas, when my entire family would share this special time together. We all still get together, but it's not the same without my mother and father.

I'm so grateful to my husband, daughters, and extended family for their unconditional love and understanding and for reminding me that tears come from happiness as well as from sorrow. Families need to make new memories so they can look to the future instead of the past and anticipate new wonders rather than dwell on the elephant in the room.

Those were difficult times, but from the vantage point of many years, I have come to see that those were joyful times, too. The turmoil of the moment can blind us to the bigger picture. When I look back, I realize I was given the opportunity to bond closer than ever with my parents, as we all knew that our time together was limited. I also received many gifts of joy from friends and colleagues who spent a great deal of time with me. They were a godsend. They helped me get through each and every day. The best way I can repay them is to do the same for others.

As grief heals with the passing of the years, and time blurs the details, we mostly remember the impressions. My parents gave me life, and I cherish the time I had with them. They left me with so many memories. I wanted so many more. We're never prepared to lose our loved ones. It's tragic when we realize only too late how much people meant to us. We need to cultivate our joy in the good years to see us through the troubled ones.

The happenings and happenstance of our lives are intertwined. With sadness comes a fringe of joy—and with joy, a touch of sadness. By experiencing each, we gain perspectives on both. The loss of my mother shook my soul, but it opened the door to a deeper relationship with my father. Without the former, I would never have experienced the latter. I have learned that things happen for a reason.

This I know: my parents gave me the gifts that I keep in my heart. They had very little for most of their lives, but what they gave me has been far more significant than money. They instilled in me the desire to reach out and to give back. My family, friends, and colleagues provided so much support and hope along the way. Without their comfort, support, and guidance I would not have had the courage to share my story. We need to build such a community, such an extended family, to see us through both good times and bad.

Each of us is on a journey. I know that mine has made me a much better person. I am thankful for the opportunities I've had. It hasn't all been wonderful, but it's the nature of a journey to encounter both peaks and valleys. We must stop to appreciate the view and not just drive on by.

Somewhere a birth, somewhere a death. In the end, our best measure of success will be that we were able to say goodbye, let go, and hold the memories deep in our hearts so that they help us along our path. We never have to walk alone, and we only have to reach for a memory to bring a smile.

INTRODUCTION
DO YOU LIVE A DRIVE-BY LIFE?

Most would agree that time seems to speed on, with seasons passing in a blur. Each year I am so surprised at how quickly birthdays roll around. As we celebrate our family birthdays, it is hard to believe how much older we are all getting.

I often wonder how much of our time we actually enjoy and how much we just while away. Have you ever experienced arriving at work or an appointment and not really knowing how you got there? You can't recall any of the landmarks along the way—as if your car was driving itself. It's a scary feeling.

The year or so before I retired, I found my days were filled with many meetings. Each day appeared to start early and finish late, and it felt as if I had done little more than make long to-do lists at those meetings. On such days, I often wondered what had happened to the joy and purpose in my life. While I enjoyed what I was doing, there was never any time to really stop and take stock of what I was accomplishing, and days became repetitive. There was no filling up of my soul—just lots of giving out.

I love to listen to the song "I Lived" by One Republic. This is the chorus:

I did it all
I owned every second that this world could give
I saw so many places, the things that I did
With every broken bone, I swear I lived

In those days, I felt that if I was really going to live, I needed to do it all. I felt I must not squander opportunities before my time ran out. Sometimes, great loss pushes a soul to do more and more, and it can make one vulnerable to living a drive-by life, becoming too busy to truly appreciate it.

But, after living with so many memories that were traumatic—illnesses, surgeries, deaths—I was determined that the last part of my life's memories would be positive.

With the right music, we either forget everything that is bothering us and enjoy the moment, or we remember everything. Music can delight the heart. It can be therapeutic and is often used that way. I believe that music is a gift, and often the lyrics in a song can speak to us in a way that provides great comfort.

Throughout my life, others have offered me that kind of comfort—their voices music in my ears as they reassured me that everything would be all right. I realize now that it will always be so, come what may. Life is fragile, as I have seen repeatedly, and yet we can take comfort in knowing we are there for one another. Sometimes we just know—we can sense, even when a situation seems impossible to overcome—that tomorrow will be better.

Still, we need to appreciate what we have today. If you are living a drive-by life, only you can make the appropriate changes. After all, you are in the driver's seat. Quantity of activity does not equal quality of activity. Busy people, who have a choice of many opportunities to pursue, must be careful to choose the ones that enhance their lives and the lives of others. Yes, you feel a compelling need to accomplish so much, but think of those around you—what do they need?

COUNTING IT AS JOY

My own family has had its share of tribulations—times when I wondered how much we could bear. It was about a year after my mother died that we began to face a series of ongoing challenges. First, my husband was seriously injured in a fall, and then our daughter developed a serious and chronic health issue.

Again we got through it, as so many families do, and we are stronger for it and much more grateful for what we have. We have learned to live and adapt to the things we cannot change. The challenges that rock our core either make us stronger or break us. It's basically up to us whether we want to make it work. Life so often can be disappointing and unfair; however, it is how we take responsibility and move forward that makes the difference.

Such times can truly test family bonds. We can be hardest on the ones we love because we know they love us unconditionally. I have learned not to be as hard on my family when I am feeling down or in despair. I no longer ask those questions "Why me?" and "Why us?" I understand that instead of lamentations, we must open our lives to seek the opportunities we will surely be given. Whether at home or in the workplace, the "team" must reassess its approach and adjust to whatever circumstances change its dynamics. Our health issues were just another experience that brought our family closer together. We are not perfect and have ongoing challenges like all families. We pull together in times of need and make things work no matter how tricky the family dynamics are at the time. I know I can make a call to any of my siblings at any time of the night or day, and they will be there for me and vice versa. I have friends with whom I share the same dynamic. To know that we have that kind of support is a wonderful gift.

Joy counts for so much of what happens in life. We endure tough times, behaving as we do for better or worse, and in the end it is the strength of our relationships that see us through. I've turned a corner in my life. I know in my heart it will all work out. It's just a matter of doing the right thing at the right time to get where we need to be. I must remind myself that I need to live in the moment today and wait until tomorrow's events unfold.

During my speaking engagements, I share that people have a choice. Every day we wake up, it is a gift, and we have the choice to smile or not to smile. We have a choice to be positive or not. When we go to work, we bring that with us. We create our day. So many people have burdens in life. I've had them myself. But I have had to say, "No, I will do this the right way. I will bring my best to work today."

> Surround yourself with people who are willing to travel with you on your journey and in whom you can trust and confide.

I have learned it doesn't matter who we are or which path we've taken, there's always hope if we maintain the right attitude. It's a matter of opening our mind and heart to positive change and being willing to ask for help.

CONSIDER THIS:

Schedule a time in your busy day to take five uninterrupted minutes to do this brief exercise. What do you think of when you wake up in the morning? Consider all the wonderful opportunities around you. Create a list of them. Create a list of your current challenges. Move the most difficult ones to the bottom of the list. Focus on the positive opportunities. Look at the challenges and apply some techniques you have used successfully in the past. Reach out to someone who you know has the skills to assist you with your challenge. Ask for help.

Asking for help is a strength, not a weakness. I am now at a point in my life where I truly believe this. Often we are afraid to reach out and ask for support. All of us have dark corners where we push things away that we do not want to deal with. We make progress when we open the door and take a close look at the situation. We see we are not alone and that we don't have to face it all by ourselves. Surround yourself with people who are willing to travel with you and in whom you can trust and confide. You deserve unconditional love and respect, and sharing it will change the lives of all involved.

So much is said about "walking the talk"—a fundamental of good living. It's so important to maintain principles and high expectations, for ourselves and for others, all of which are a part of our journey to excellence. When we open ourselves to healing and show that we will do our part, we can set aside the difficulties and focus on what is worthwhile. We can let go of the problems and issues of the past to focus on the relationships with which we have been blessed.

Even in your darkest moment, you can find your way. There's always a way. The real change must begin by looking into ourselves, as we cannot control others. Instead of abandoning a relationship, why not ask yourself how you can be the one to make a difference? It is so empowering when we rise above and reach out—when we take the high road. Running from an issue prolongs the situation, which causes more anger and misery.

I've learned there are three sides to every story—yours, mine, and the truth—that is, your perception, my perception, and reality. Don't let disagreements take control of your life. Why squander hours, days, months, or years that could be spent with the people you care about? Allowing stubbornness to take over takes your personal, positive power away. If you can't let it go, then you must work it out. I know personally how easy that is to say but how hard it is to do. It takes courage and conviction, but we cannot move forward in life if we are haunted by the past.

We have so much to lose that way. We must not run away from things. If we are to run at all, then we should run toward something.

> I've learned there are three sides to every story—yours, mine, and the truth—that is, your perception, my perception, and reality.

It's far better to appreciate and live in the moment than to always look for the next great thing. It's better to live in gratitude than to try to stake out new territory all the time. It's better to stop and to love than to just drive by.

HELP ALONG THE WAY

When I find myself worrying excessively, I try to remember to focus on changing only what I can and living the best life that I can.

It always comes down to this: we can only change ourselves. Once we own our behavior and attitude, we gain real power. We can take the necessary steps at just the right time. We can step back with a clear head and ask, "How can I make this work?"

Too many people instead take the approach of, "If I'm not happy, then I'm going to make you unhappy." This approach is inappropriate and counterproductive. It hurts you, and it hurts everybody around you—and it is a huge waste of time. We have only one life, and we deserve so much better than that. Every day is a gift. Every day we're starting fresh. If we carry the past and the anger, we'll never move forward. We'll always be stepping back.

> Joy counts for so much of what happens in life. We endure tough times, behaving as we do for better or worse, and in the end it is the strength of our relationships that see us through.

In his book *Hide Your Goat*, Steve Gilliland[1] writes that we need the courage to recognize who we are. Each day when we wake up, we need to summon the courage to do the things we need to do. We need to live for today instead of worrying so much about tomorrow and what might happen. And we need to do so with a humble heart. We must learn humility.

Each of us holds the power. If you are willing to consider a change, then it can happen. You might not buy into the change right away, but at least think about it. Consider the possibility. Otherwise, you will never take the first step.

Sometimes we get in a rut. We feel we cannot get out—and that is when we need to ask for help. Whether it's a professional, a friend or someone you deeply trust, people are waiting for you to reach out to them. There is always somebody who will listen and who has knowledge to share with you. Wisdom is there for those who seek it.

A CULTURE OF CARING

Personally, I feel I have led a privileged life because of my parents and the way I was reared. My parents had their years of struggle, yet they were so generous. They worked hard most of their lives, and it wasn't until their later years that fortune smiled on them—but the hard work and dedication to family and friends *did* pay off.

We are all blessed in one way or another. Often we don't realize how fortunate we are because we focus on the negative, not the positive. If we start the day with a glass half full instead of half empty, we are sure to look at things differently.

In that spirit, I want to give back as much as I can. I've heard people say we should "give until it hurts," but it never hurts. It feels right. My life is far from perfect, but I'm here, and I have so much. I feel privileged to be able to do what I do and to still be on this earth with the love that surrounds me.

Sometimes we have to walk the path before we get the message and before we learn. We all experience life differently, and so our paths will differ—and we must be compassionate of others while they are on their journey. This can be difficult for people like myself who have limited patience, but this, too, can be practiced.

Sometimes when I hear people saying they have to get their life in order due to a health scare, I think, "Well, your life should be in order already. Ideally, we should be living the life we want and not just reacting to some scare of the moment. Tomorrow isn't promised. If this was your last day—and none of us knows for certain that it isn't—would you be content with your state of affairs? Joy and sadness attend us all, but by which will you live? Life can be over at the snap of a finger. Did you make the most of it? Did you do your best with the time you were given here, or did you just drive by?

CONSIDER THIS:

Do you have your life in order?

If today were your last day on earth, would you be content?

How would you put your life in order?

We need to be careful we're not so busy that we don't stop to appreciate what matters. Somewhere in the ebb and flow, there must be time to reflect. *Carpe diem*—we must seize the moment. We need to develop an appreciation for what we have now and not lose that perspective in the face of things that really don't matter. Instead of regrets, why not experience gratitude for having shared our time together well? Consider what matters most to you, and what might matter most to those around you. If you weren't happy yesterday, try a new approach today. Never be trapped—you and those around you deserve far better.

The circumstances of my life have shaped me into who I am today—and for that I am thankful. That doesn't mean I don't wish things could have been different, but I accept who I am, the path I have walked, and I am prepared for the journey ahead even if I find it daunting. I have faced many challenges and have even felt sorry for myself at times, but I understand how surviving challenges strengthens us and paves the way to success. I've always been able to come through and rise above adversity. It has not been easy, but I look to the future and try not to dwell on negatives from the past, because that really brings me down and prevents me from living in the moment. Negativity can bring us down so quickly. We must be vigilant and push it out of our minds.

Each of us should be on a journey to excellence, seeking to enhance the quality of both our own lives and the lives of those with whom we interact. This journey does not mean we are expected to be perfect, but it involves self-reflection and striving to be the best we can be. We must be more than drive-by observers. We are meant to actively make a difference in the lives of others.

Each chapter of this book is about one aspect of the journey of life. Together, these aspects become an irrepressible force compelling us to give back, to the best of our ability. They add up to a culture of caring that can permeate our lives—in our families, in our work-places, and in all of our dealings with others along the way.

JOY

CHAPTER ONE

Joy does not simply happen to us.
We have to choose joy and keep choosing it every day.
—Henri Nouwen

A re you looking for joy on your daily journey?

We all experience joy differently, but it is often the little things that bring us the most happiness. As human beings, we need to celebrate joyful simplicities that bring comfort and well-being— this should be among our highest priorities.

Just before I summoned the courage to retire, I bought a new car. I have never been much of a car person; in fact, I've never really even noticed car brands. All I've ever needed or wanted was a good, dependable car to get around in.

But strangely enough, I found a car that I really connect with, and it brought me so much pleasure that I named it Joy. My youngest daughter had a good laugh when she heard me refer to the car by that name. I can hardly blame her—it seems strange to me, too. We had always driven a van or an SUV, convenient for the kids, but this time it would be something different.

My journey with Joy began one day when I was at a fundraising event for our local hospice, where I served on the board. The hospice was raffling a BMW car. I slid into the seat—and I felt transformed.

"I love the car, but it's not necessary for me," I said to my board colleague and friend, who'd developed the raffle through the local BMW dealership where he worked. "It's more than I need."

But I just couldn't stop thinking about that car. My husband and I talked it over, and we decided to buy one just like it, and once I was behind the wheel I knew it was the right choice. I felt warmth in my heart. "I'm going to name it Joy," I said to my friend, and he told me that "joy" is actually used by BMW in its advertising.

And now I smile whenever I'm in my car. I feel very safe in it. As things go through my mind in my car—all the wonderful things I have, all the opportunities—sometimes tears run down my face. It's as if something special is there with me in the car. I think I see my car as a symbol of my courage to let go and to open my life to change. Sometimes we have to stop doing what is familiar and comfortable so that we can open ourselves to new opportunities for joy.

I put on my music and drive down the road, and I am free. I find great pleasure in music. It's a wonderful tool for bringing joy into my life—the car, the music, the road ahead—the pleasure is not in the material possession but in the feelings that it conjures.

For most of my life, as far back as I can remember, giving back has brought me great joy. I even found the connection to my car through giving back; I met my friend through my service on the hospice board. We found we shared similar values, and he and his family have become an important part of my family's life.

I was also deeply impressed by the dedication of the BMW dealership, Budds' BMW, for developing the raffle with the hospice. This is a family-owned business that truly knows how to practice excellence and give back to its community. Over the last few years, I have been so impressed by the way the staff and leadership have reached out and provided support to so many local organizations, practicing excellence in everything they do. I am always drawn to people who give back. I am interested in building relationships, and out of this experience have come long-term family friends who share our commitment to community. I went to this dealership because I knew they were people who give back to others, and it came full circle. Joy came back to me.

Steve Gilliland writes in his book, *Enjoy the Ride*, "You will never leave where you are, until you decide where you would rather be."[2] My car represents that sentiment for me. I was ready for a career change and was deciding where I would rather be. This was a turning point in my life—I was heading in a new direction.

CONSIDER THIS:

Are you where you want to be today?

What are your plans for tomorrow?

If you were given an opportunity to make a change at work, what would it be?

If you were given an opportunity to make a change in your personal life, what would it be?

Where is your next destination in your journey of life?

THE MUSIC OF THE HEART

I recently traveled to Florida to be with a dear friend who had suddenly taken ill. He was in critical condition and was fighting to survive. During most of the time I spent with him, his wife, and his brother-in-law, it was a frightening experience, but I held onto hope that he would survive. I was so thankful when it became clear that our prayers were answered and my friend would recover. This visit was very meaningful and brought more clarity to my life. I learned how important our relationship meant to me and how important a role my friend had played in my life for more than 25 years. On the morning I was to return home, I sat on the balcony and gazed out at the ocean—I find that water provides me with insight, inspiration, and energy. The melody and lyrics to Josh Groban's "You Raise Me Up" drifted through my mind. I played that song and listened intently.

There are times when we are down and we are weary, and we need something to lift us up. My friend's life was still hanging in the balance, and I wasn't ready to let him go. I needed that song at that moment to give me the strength to fly back home, knowing in my heart he would recover.

When I think about that song I also think about my parents, and the guidance they gave me. But when they were guiding me in my life, I didn't really appreciate it or embrace what they were doing for me. Only later did I remember their words and actions.

"I am strong when I am on your shoulders. You raise me up to more than I can be." The words assure us that we can endure the stormy seas and make it to the mountaintop. With the help of others, we can be more than we can be when we are alone.

Whenever I think of that song, I feel encouraged and stronger. I will never give up. My eldest daughter asks me, "Mom, why do you play that song so much? It makes me so sad." It is interesting how music means different things to different people. Each of us is drawn to music depending on our needs at the time.

"It makes me so happy," I say. I've pulled so many wonderful things from that song. It has given me strength, and it motivates me to go on. Music evokes memories—and has the capacity to flood us with joy. Good lyrics soak into the soul and refresh it.

Along the way, people have come and gone and entered my heart for good. In this, it's often the little things that matter, sometimes immensely. For example, a friend who is an accomplished pianist spent hours learning and practicing that song for me. He went out of his way, and he knew he was making a difference for me. I'm sure he could see on my face just how much it meant to me.

I think of the words of Mahatma Gandhi, "Be the change you want to see in the world." It doesn't take much to touch the lives of others and to inject some joy into their day. A smile, a quick phone call, an email, or even a text message to let someone know we are thinking about them—those simple things can mean so much. Today's technology can be considered negative at times, and certainly it can be abused when it's substituted for face time, but it also holds the power to connect people's hearts in ways never before possible. Used wisely, with the right balance, technology can spread the joy far and wide.

In his article "7 Morning Rituals to Empower Your Day and Change Your Life," Gilbert Ross suggests there are things we can do each day to positively change our lives.[3] He recommends that we listen to uplifting music in the morning before work, and even during our commute, to help us have a more positive outlook on our day (and we might want to stay away from the news and sad music as we start our day). Preselecting and downloading motivational music can prepare us for a challenging meeting, appointment, or test.

THE MOMENTS OF WONDER

Sometimes I sit and close my eyes and rewind my day, striving to recall the moments of wonder. I don't want to let them escape me; it upsets me to think that might happen. I want to savor the joyous moments and appreciate the people who gave them to me.

These are the practitioners of joy, and they deserve my gratitude. I feel an obligation to recognize them and to give back. We can do it simply with a warm welcome to those we encounter throughout the day or by taking a moment to hold the door and smile. Once, these were basic good manners and felt natural, and we need to get back to them.

In the waiting room at a hospital recently, I was sitting near a woman who was feeling anxious about a test she was waiting for. She really wanted to talk to me, and I really wanted to read my book, but finally I closed my book and just chatted with her for a little bit, until I was called in for my appointment.

That woman was reaching out for support. She just needed a little bit of attention. I thought, "One day I'm going to feel that I need it, too, so I'm going to give it to her now." It took so little to brighten her day. Our paths might never cross again, so why waste such an opportunity? Someday, in my moment of anxiety, I will want someone to brighten mine.

Meanwhile, another woman had been audibly complaining. "They told me to get here early, and for what? Just to sit here waiting? I'm tired. If they don't want to take care of old people, they should just line them up and shoot them."

I could see how she was affecting those near her, who seemed to be studying the floor at their feet. Life is too short for that kind of attitude. Our time is best spent in raising people up, not bringing them down. Our most worthwhile time occurs when we find the joy amid the turmoil. Look for the shining star—it is out there.

During our workday, we are often surrounded by those who are not joyful or grateful and who can be very draining if we allow it. Sometimes it is better to say nothing if we have nothing positive to say and to just ignore negative or inappropriate behavior that may end on its own anyway, without creating drama or further distress. But there are times when we have to speak up and share our truths because it is the right

"Be the change you want to see in the world."

thing to do. Of course, when we do intervene or speak up, timing is everything, and we may need support to know when and how to do that. But it is not acceptable to allow others to consistently try to steal our joy.

> Our time is best spent in raising people up, not bringing them down.

Sometimes the people we work with need a little attention or support. Perhaps they don't know how to ask, so they may do something that could be considered irritating to get our attention. The best thing one can do is to reach out and take a moment to support someone in need. This must be done in moderation, as your primary goal is to fulfill your work responsibilities, but subscribing to this may lessen some of those day-to-day work issues.

CONSIDER THIS:

Think of the colleagues you work with. Is there an individual or a small group you may be able to reach out to and brighten their day?

You may want to start by doing something for one person or for everyone if it's a small group. What you do could be as simple as bringing in a special something to eat. Observe the response.

THE UNEXPECTED GIFTS

Early in my career, I enjoyed anonymously sending people bouquets of flowers once a month. There was always somebody who needed a lift. Someone might be caring for a sick relative; someone else might be going through a divorce. I did this for a while, and nobody ever figured out who the bouquets came from, which was really important to me—I've found that a level of mystery makes the receivers consider the possibilities of who might care enough to think of them. Later in my career I sent out Lindt chocolate bars to various people around my workplace, and I sent out cards that were humorous or musical or that just said, "Have a great day!" Most everyone loves surprises.

People were always trying to figure out who the mysterious benefactor might be. It became their quest, and I found it amusing. Is kindness such a rarity that people wonder who in the world would do such a thing?

The cumulative effect of raising people's spirits even a little bit every day is huge. Most people are appreciative and can see the value of this but don't take the time. They are too busy with their drive-by lives and think they will do it tomorrow; they go through the motions, doing the same things every day and getting the same outcomes. Instead, they could easily make a few changes. Maybe they could enter by a different door and meet someone new, and hold the door for that person, or pick up an extra cup of tea on their way to work, or put a chocolate on someone's desk. It's the unexpected that's the biggest gift and brings the most joy. This kind of giving is so simple, and the benefits are immeasurable.

The more I give, and the more I do things for others, the greater joy I feel. Our gift comes back to us—and through the act of giving, our heart gets bigger. It is often observed that people don't care how much we know until they know how much we care.

MAKING THE DIFFERENCE

Susan Smith Jones' book, *The Joy Factor*,[4] has been an inspiration for me. She writes about setting the bar high and choosing to live your best life. "You have this power within you—it is the birthright and potential of every human being," she says, "The only possible limitation is your own thought, belief, and imagination."

Those are words to take to heart: The good life is our birthright, and we have the right to pursue it. We need to set our standards high.

> It's the unexpected that's the biggest gift and truly brings the most joy.

"We know what we are, but know not what we may be," Shakespeare wrote in *Hamlet*. We should reach for the stars in our quest to find out all that we might be.

Get over yourself, get over your challenges, and step back. Ask yourself: "What can I do to make the difference in someone's life? What can I do today, no matter how small?" When I started to practice that simple exercise, I began to feel real joy in my heart. It takes but moments a day to do so much, and it is so much fun to consider the small things we can do to make a difference. Remember, it doesn't take a lot of money or things; it just takes a moment to think of something special that will bring someone joy.

GRATITUDE

CHAPTER TWO

Gratitude, like faith, is a muscle.
The more you use it, the stronger it grows…
—Alan Cohen

Are you practicing gratitude?

There is a lot to be said for starting your day the right way. Taking a positive step out of bed each day will set your path in the right direction. The stress in our daily lives can easily overtake without us realizing it. Gilbert Ross says, "The real power of gratitude is that it makes you pick out and focus on what is working in your life." He reinforces that "quite often we pick out the pain points, the problems, the bottlenecks, whatever it is that is not working in our life and causing friction, anxiety, and unhappiness. This is like constantly rewriting the script of your life with a negative or tragic overtone. Your subconscious mind follows faithfully that script you write whether it is a negative or positive one."[5]

Clearly we need to place our attention on the things that are going well to help us through the challenges of each day. Practicing gratitude from the moment we wake up can truly make a difference.

CONSIDER THIS:

Each morning, set your alarm to wake you up 15 minutes earlier than you need to, to allow yourself time to practice gratitude and to focus on the positive aspects of your previous day, week, and life in general. This may be the best 15 minutes of your day. Ensure you take time to fine-tune the rest of your waking hours.

On a recent vacation, I took only one book with me—*What I Know For Sure* by Oprah Winfrey.[6] I love to read when I travel, and I might read three to five books over a week's vacation. There was something in this book that grabbed me and held on tight. I related to so much in that book—the joys and the sorrows. I read it more than once, with tears running down my face.

Sometimes, Oprah writes, we get so focused on the difficulty of our climb that we lose sight of being grateful for simply having the mountain that we are climbing. We take a lot of what we have in our life for granted. We lack gratitude. The book quotes the 13th century German philosopher Meister Eckhart, "If the only prayer you ever say in your entire life is 'thank you,' it will be enough." How simple and yet so profound. Where are the T-shirts with *that* saying?

For me, it is a privilege to go to work every day. Before I left my career at Mohawk College, where I basically grew up, I certainly saw my work as a privilege, because I was given so many opportunities. I moved from a support staff role to a faculty role and finished my career in a variety of administrative roles. Back then, these opportunities were seldom available. If you were support staff, you stayed in that category for your career. I am thankful that things have changed—though slowly. I was given the chance to prove myself, and I never took that for granted. I feel so grateful for that.

I was 20 years old when I began my career, the same year I was married. It felt as if I worked at the same organization forever, wearing so many different hats. How many chances do we get to have so many career opportunities? I was very fortunate. I was in the right place with the right leadership and the right people, and I was willing. I strived for excellence, as my parents had modeled for me. When people see that—when they see you bringing your best to work—they want to help you. When they see you're a positive person and you're smiling, they want to be part of your team.

When I spoke at my retirement parties, I had tears of gratitude in my eyes. In the months before, as that day drew closer, I came to clearly understand how much my work family meant to me. I knew then that this place would always be my home, no matter where I went. I was part of it, and it was part of me.

At times during my career, I felt disappointed with people who became negative when something didn't go their way. We had numerous leadership changes over the years, and it created a great deal of anxiety and dissension. In that kind of environment, those who align themselves with negative people find it's really tough to shake them later. People need to make a conscious decision when faced with change—will you embrace the change positively or view it as negative? If we are at odds with the system, going to work every day can become more of a challenge. Instead of getting our work done, we find ways not to do the work. It won't feel like a privilege. "All the new people are changing things," some of my colleagues would complain. I would say, "Things have to change or we will never grow as an organization." People and institutions change and grow, just as a child learns and builds for a future. To me, it just makes sense. The longer things stay the same, the older they become, and the less opportunity for growth.

I was excited to see change, and I wanted to be part of it. Work should be enjoyable, and our jobs should be stimulating. That's why I got involved on committees, and it's why I ran for the board of governors. I felt it was my obligation to get involved and give 100 percent. I wanted to be a part of change that would keep my workplace strong and relevant.

> "If the only prayer you ever say in your entire life is 'thank you,' it will be enough."

Transitions can be difficult for everyone, and it is normal to resist change, but we must embrace the possibility that change will actually enhance our workplace and our lives.

RECOGNIZING THE BENEFITS

It saddened me to see so many people did not feel that sense of gratitude. Some seemed to feel they were owed something, either by their employer or by life itself. Some developed a sense of entitlement. In truth, we are "owed" only for the job we are doing at the moment. We all forget that at times.

It's a special gift to work at a place where we receive numerous benefits and opportunities for growth. We need to cherish it. Our attitude plays a significant role in how we perceive our employment and whether we think of those benefits as a gift or an entitlement.

CONSIDER THIS:

Give yourself the "Gratitude Reality Check." Send a quick email to ten friends or relatives and ask these questions:

- What work benefits do you receive?
- What is the financial value of those benefits?

The responses may surprise you. You may find many people won't be able to answer these questions in full. Upon investigating, they might be surprised to see what they actually receive in benefits. Sometimes we go to work each day and become part of a routine that doesn't allow us to stop and consider our surroundings. Our pay cheques are deposited into our bank accounts, and most, if not all, the money is already spent to pay our bills. Unless we lose our jobs or become ill, we often take for granted the benefits of our employment.

When I decided to move on, I sought the services of a career coach. This was a great gift. This opportunity meant so much to me.

As my coach helped me transition into my new world, retirement had not been high on my list of priorities, but I had come to realize it was time for a change. I had so much more I wanted to do—and I wanted to do it well.

PRACTICING GIVING THANKS

During my coaching, I was introduced to many new things, and one of them was gratitude. We began with a book written by Wendy Meg Siegel called *The Gratitude Habit*. "Thanksgiving is more than a holiday that comes once a year," Siegel says, and she talks about what thanksgiving truly is—what it means to be grateful.[7]

When I was growing up, we sat around the dinner table every day and listened, learned, and talked. Sometimes it seems that it's only at the Thanksgiving dinner table people talk about the things for which they are grateful. We need to find the time to have thanksgiving every day.

"Cultivating your relationship with gratitude," Siegel writes, "is a simple path to improving the quality of your life and experiencing more joy and happiness every day." Gratitude leads to joy, which leads again to gratitude. And how does Siegel define gratitude? It is "a feeling of appreciation for all that you have in your life and all that you are. It is the expression of thanksgiving for the things that make life worth living and for the hidden blessings that are often overlooked. It's being able to say thank you for the little things that make you smile and for those that add joy to living."

Gratitude has to be practiced. It is not innate. How do you practice it? Just look around you. Are you thankful for your family? Are you thankful for your home? Are you thankful for the basic things that keep you alive every day? When I was living a drive-by life, I wasn't practicing gratitude. Now, I'm much more appreciative and excited about how wonderful my life is and about all these new things that I'm reading and practicing.

It's easy to say, "stop and smell the roses," but it's not as easy to apply that advice. You have to develop that in your life. Sometimes it comes through adversity. The difficult things in your life can help you obtain a perspective on the good things you have. Consider whether you are truly grateful; you won't know until you take a close look at yourself. Once you feel it, you will want to reach out to help others—starting with a smile and progressing all the way to serving the community. You will want to make a difference.

This isn't so much about sending food to the third world but rather about deciding each and every day whether we will support others with kindness and a smile. So many of us have been given so much. We must embrace life, recognize our bounty, and share it.

Sometimes we think it has to be something really huge to make us happy. But we're heading into a downward spiral when we need things to make us happy. Instead, we can be grateful for the smallest of gestures and experiences that each day brings us.

ON THE JOB AND OFF

On the job and off, it's important to recognize others and to thank them. In our lives, and particularly in our workplaces, we often fail to do that. People who feel unappreciated are less likely to try very hard. They may develop a negative attitude.

It's the touches we can make in people's lives that let them know we appreciate them. When people know they're appreciated, they will work that much harder to do things for us, and to be the best they can be. Otherwise they may do less. I'm not saying that's right—I'm just saying that's real.

Roy Saunderson, an employee recognition authority, points out that the traditional Christmas bonus has come to be seen as a relic of the past. It's not typical today.[8] Still, it's good style for a company to show gratitude to the employees in some manner at the end of each year. He suggests ways managers can end the work year with good employee rapport. Frankly, ending the year that way is far from enough. Good engagement requires a lot more.

Saunderson emphasizes regularly sharing thank you's. When we do, we will go far toward improving retention, and we will encourage high productivity. Expressions of gratitude should be delivered daily. There has to be a way to let people know every day that their contributions make a difference to us and to the company.

I recommend giving someone a card or sending a quick email. Or send them a chocolate bar—a little surprise. Put a flower on their desk, or offer tickets to a special event. It doesn't have to be big. It just needs to communicate, "I'm thinking about you. I appreciate you." On the job, let your coworkers know you appreciate them and you are all in it together—as they say, there is no "I" in the word "team."

A little appreciation can go a long way toward changing someone's day. Sometimes, in our fast-paced, drive-by existence, we are all too ready to take shortcuts. If the shortcuts include forgetting to share your gratitude with others, then those around you are likely to feel unappreciated.

"Never neglect to say thank you," Saunderson says, "no matter what you give." The expression of gratitude is as important as the gift. One-on-one meetings with the boss can mean so much, for example. If the boss can spend just a few minutes with each employee expressing gratitude, you can be sure that attitudes will change. These meetings need to be genuine, of course; people know when we're sincere and when we're not. When we try to say thank you, is the response a hearty "you're welcome" or a curt "no problem"? That can speak volumes about people's perception of us.

> Expressions of gratitude should be delivered daily to make a significant difference.

When facilitating employee engagement seminars, we recommend training staff and managers at different levels—and it all starts with developing the attitude that work is a privilege. It's something we get to do, not something that we have to do. Employees will start to feel that way—and will be more successful—when they see management cares about them and their contributions. Too often, supervisors don't appear to put any effort into sharing their appreciation with employees, even though they could do it so easily.

A small gesture can cultivate a great deal of gratitude and spirit. If it takes a whole lot more to touch people's hearts, then the problem might be greater than you think. A bonus is nice, but you have to do more than throw money at a problem. What you need to express is appreciation. Real gratitude shines. It shines from your body, your face, and just the way you walk. It's like a beacon, and we all need it to help us find the way.

CONSIDER THIS:

Using the chart below, make a list each morning or evening for one week of ten things that you are grateful for, without repeating any items.

You may be surprised at how many things you take for granted each day. After you complete your list at the end of the week, consider what items on the list you would not like to live without.

Quite often it is the simple things that bring us the greatest joy.

TODAY I AM GRATEFUL FOR...

MONDAY	
1.	6.
2.	7.
3.	8.
4.	9.
5.	10.

TUESDAY	
1.	6.
2.	7.
3.	8.
4.	9.
5.	10.

WEDNESDAY

1.	6.
2.	7.
3.	8.
4.	9.
5.	10.

THURSDAY

1.	6.
2.	7.
3.	8.
4.	9.
5.	10.

FRIDAY

1.	6.
2.	7.
3.	8.
4.	9.
5.	10.

SATURDAY

1.	6.
2.	7.
3.	8.
4.	9.
5.	10.

SUNDAY

1.	6.
2.	7.
3.	8.
4.	9.
5.	10.

OPTIMISM

CHAPTER THREE

A pessimist sees the difficulty in every opportunity;
an optimist sees the opportunity in every difficulty.
—Winston S. Churchill

D o you consider yourself an optimistic person?

Do you work with optimistic people?

As my children grew up, I often shared with them the story of "The Little Engine That Could." It made them smile when they were small and roll their eyes when they got older, but I think they realized there was truth in the old story. Giving up is easier, at first, than working hard to succeed.

Many times I told my daughters they could be anything they wanted in life if they were willing to work hard for it. Often they achieved their goals, but when they did not, it was quite evident they didn't really want what they thought they wanted. Determination can bring out the best in us and help us succeed.

I often think back to the advice my father gave when he knew I was facing difficult challenges at work. "Never give up," he told me. His words live on, because I tell my daughters the same thing. I believe it takes great courage to find one's passion—to know when it is time to move on so that we can be the best we can be. It's so easy to give up and give in and stay put. That's stagnation.

Leaving a job that was part of my life for so long and that defined so much of me was hard to do. It was probably one of the hardest decisions I ever had to make and one I did not take lightly. Over a period of several years, a voice inside me was constantly challenging me and asking if it was really my destiny to stay at one institution for my entire career.

There were compelling reasons to stay and just as many reasons to leave. "Are you crazy?" some people asked me, "You're leaving a job like that? Why would you do that?"

"Because my life is more important to me than that," I responded. I knew there were other things I needed to accomplish.

I knew my future was more secure if I stayed, but I also knew I couldn't stay at a job where I was no longer challenged. Understanding that there needs to be a balance between emotional and intellectual growth, I equate passion with optimism. To be optimistic, we have to be passionate. What's the opposite of optimism? Pessimism. There are many things in life to feel bad about. Each of us has struggles. Things bring us down. At that point in my life, I didn't want to step backward into regrets. I wanted to step forward into a balanced period of growth, both emotionally and intellectually.

The antidote to pessimism is to look forward to something. Be passionate about what you do. When you go to work every day and it feels like just a job, it's time to consider a change. You need to listen to your heart and pursue what you are good at doing, not just what is easy for you. Without a challenge, you lose passion, and then you lose optimism. When you get into a rut or life becomes an unproductive routine and you let healthy habits fall by the wayside—things can become monotonous, and you can lose motivation and self-confidence.

> Getting over this fear will not only give you more confidence but will also give you the momentum to take things to the next level and get more out of life.

Don't get stuck in a sea of sameness. Keep pressing forward. You have to change things up from time to time to keep your momentum and to continue your personal growth.

You have to listen to your heart, and you have to know what's right for you. You have to be ready and willing to change. You have to continue to dream. If you are at a time in your life when you're struggling and you're not feeling optimistic, start looking back to a time when you were.

CONSIDER THIS:

What brought you joy when you were young?

What made you happy then?

What made you happy a few months or a year ago, when things were really good in your life?

Get back in touch with what motivated you then.

Consider today's possibilities and opportunities, and begin to dream again.

Many people let fear set their path. After years in one career, they may feel they want to do other things in life, but they have a really good job and make good money, so they just stay where they are. Anything else would be too risky. What if they fail? Fear can paralyze people, robbing them of the pursuit of things that might be. It sucks away their optimism. They end up staying in the same place, stuck in mediocrity. That place might feel safer, but it's dangerous in that it drains the spirit and wastes human potential. Getting over this fear will not only give you more confidence but will also give you the momentum to take things to the next level and get more out of life.

> Be willing to give it all you have, because it may take all you have to succeed. In the end, when you have obtained what you really wanted, the effort will have been worth it.

Optimism will propel you to greater heights. That's the lesson here. To me, it's common sense. To make a difference, we need courage, yet many people cannot overcome their fear of risk.

If you are in a job and it's not working for you, don't draw it out. Admit you need a change, learn from the experience, and then move forward to demonstrate what you have learned. It's okay to make mistakes. That's how we learn. We learn and grow because we realize what didn't work.

I agree with the sentiment that pain is temporary, but quitting is forever. Never give up. Sometimes we do need to move on when we have learned all that we can in a particular role, but moving on is part of growth.

It's okay to fall down on the road. It is not the falling but how we pick ourselves up and recover that reveals the kind of person we are and how quickly we will grow. Stand strong and push forward. Have faith. We never know what is waiting around the corner. Each step forward will make us stronger.

> Pain is temporary, but giving up and quitting is forever.

A BALM TO HEALTH AND SPIRIT

When you choose optimism, your attitude changes—toward failure, toward your setbacks, toward the frustrating things that happen in the course of the day. You even come to understand there is a reason for everything. It's a principle for living—things are interconnected, and when one door closes, another opens. Be willing to give it all you have, because it may take all you have to succeed. In the end, when you have obtained what you really wanted, the effort will have been worth it.

Optimism comes with demonstrated health benefits. Often we hear about people who have been diagnosed with cancer and whose attitude helps them to live longer and adds to their quality of life. They have a reason to live. How many times have we heard of people who gave up the struggle and died? I have personally witnessed this within my family. Sometimes there's a time to submit to the inevitable. When strength fails, and the time comes, you will know. But the spirit of "I will live" will increase your chances of enduring longer exponentially.

Relationships thrive on optimism. It's an attitude that draws people to you. Negative people try to pull you down to their level. Most of us want to be near those who raise us up.

CHOOSE YOUR FRIENDS WISELY

The late Jim Rohn, an entrepreneur and motivational author, wrote that we are the average of the five people we spend the most time with.[9] I take that to mean we must choose our friends wisely. Do you want to associate with those who bring you down, or do you want to be near those who build you up and inspire you?

> Relationships thrive on optimism. It's an attitude that draws people to you. Negative people try to pull you down to their level. Most of us want to be near those who raise us up.

I choose to be around people who share my values and people I aspire to be like. They do the things I believe are important. "My inner circle of friends and my mother keep me on track," Steve Gilliland says in *Enjoy the Ride*.[10] I grew up with strong values, and it is to those values that I have always returned. My parents had high expectations, and, in turn, I pass those high expectations on to my children.

I'm willing to change. I'm always willing to listen, and I appreciate constructive criticism, but I'm a great debater—so if you're going to take me on, you'd better have your facts. That's just the way I am. I want to be open, but I also know when to stop. I know when it's my time to listen.

The people around us are so important to who we are and to what and how we achieve. We may need to let some friends go. It's hard to do, but we need to consider how compatible they are with our values. It's not our job to tell people what we see as their shortcomings. We won't singlehandedly change them. We don't have that power, but we do have the power to be the person we want to be. If we spend time around people who are averse to our values, we run the risk of becoming more like them. And, fair or not, we will also be judged by the company we keep.

A child growing up will take on family values if he or she spends time with the family. Children pick up the values, positive or negative, of those with whom they spend time. Sometimes young people get into bad crowds because they lack the guidance and

> The late Jim Rohn, an entrepreneur and motivational author, wrote that we are the average of the five people we spend the most time with.

values of strong role models. Often they are looking to belong, and sometimes the choices they make are not the best ones. Don't be afraid to disappoint those who would force you into their box as a condition for accepting you. Be sure your decisions are based on strong, positive values.

To become such role models for young people is how we can create optimism in a world that often is sorely lacking in it. That's how you reach out and say, "You're important to me. I have time for you." A pessimist can be poison to people in need. You might be the only person who someone can approach for help. You might be the only spirit who will be there to raise them up. You never know when you will become somebody's lifeline.

> If we spend time around people who are averse to our values, we run the risk of becoming more like them. And, fair or not, we will also be judged by the company we keep.

EXCELLENCE

CHAPTER FOUR

Excellence is the gradual result of always striving to do better.
—Pat Riley

Do you practice excellence in your work and personal life?

"Virtues are formed in man by his doing the actions," Aristotle wrote. When we do the right things, he taught, we can achieve the virtue of excellence. In other words, excellence is a habit.

Excellence is a way of life that requires inimitable passion and energy. The journey to excellence is more challenging than we might think. We must put forth great effort to develop habits to be the best we can be.

In my own life, I have difficulty saying no to people. I'm a thorough planner, which is a necessary trait in the pursuit of excellence—but sometimes I plan too much. Even today, I still fill my days with more than I should. Perhaps it rolls over from my past work life. This kind of conditioning is hard to change. Constant planning propels me into a drive-by life, and I struggle daily to find balance. It is hard when we love to be busy and involved, and we enjoy new challenges and experiences. I understand that feeling of wanting to have it all—but what is the good of having it all if we are only going through the motions and not enjoying the journey?

I'm learning, with practice, to slow down. Excellence is a journey, and I believe in my heart that what is important is to be working toward it. I have crowded so many things into my life over the years that have been joyful—and yet it's important not to get to the point where one is constantly running. The pursuit of excellence is not the drive-by life. I am learning to stay present and in the moment, but it is an ongoing struggle for me. As I change my patterns, it will become easier over time.

"I'm hearing you say two things," a longtime friend told me. "Sometimes you're saying you love it all, and sometimes you're saying it's too much." And she is right—I find it so fulfilling, but I take on too much. You could say I am a work in progress. Really, that is what all of our lives are—a work in progress. Progress is good as long as we are taking more steps forward than we are backward.

The very thing I am tempted to define as "excellence"—that is, the pursuit of all these activities, saying yes to everyone—is really not excellence at all. Sometimes we need to mature into a broader definition of the word. Doing too much can spread us so thin that we're not excellent anymore. When I feel joy surging through me, I am filled with the

> All of our lives are a work in progress with no end date.

feeling that "I can do that!" But I cannot do it all, I know. The joy can be so intense it is overwhelming and leads me to lose perspective on other aspects of life.

You might say excellence requires some winnowing. We have to work on it. Self-reflection is a big part of excellence. If excellence is a journey, then part of that journey is being able to ask: How can I be better? How can I be ever more excellent? How do I model this for other people?

CONSIDER THIS:

Ask yourself the questions below to assess your journey to excellence:

- Are you passionate about being excellent?

- Do you have an inspiring goal?

- Have you developed a realistic strategy?

- Do you have a mentor?

- Are you a lifelong learner?

- Are you resilient?

- Will you continue to the end without giving up?

- Will you ask others for support along the way?

- Are you willing to work both smart and hard?

EMBRACING THE OPPORTUNITIES

On your journey to excellence, lifelong learning is important. We have to keep reading, learning, and listening. We have to want to grow, to take in more, and to be able to stay relevant with the changing world. Because I worked at an educational institution, I was part of ongoing change and development, which I found stimulating. It set the bar for my learning. Striving for excellence must be part of who we are, not just something our job requires. At times in my work, I felt like a bird soaring; in many ways, my job was like the song *Wind Beneath My Wings*.

A great deal of my learning came from getting involved in the community and on boards, and my workplace promoted that in the spirit of giving back. I took on more than was expected of me and grew so much through working with other professionals and on boards under extraordinary circumstances. I was part of a team that drew from all kinds of resources, people, and talent. I knew that through volunteering, I could make an important difference.

I participated in the opportunities presented to me. I embraced them. I knew that those experiences would make me a better person. In reflection, those experiences shaped me as an individual who has the capacity to give, who wants to give, and who has a far greater life because she can give. Volunteerism changed my life in so many ways. We learn so much from volunteering and get a great return on our investment of time. We gain hands-on knowledge and experi-

> Volunteering offers numerous learning opportunities that empower us personally, develop our civic responsibility, and inspire us to practice excellence more and more.

ence, often from professionals—something that cannot be learned in the classroom.

Anyone who volunteers grows from the experience, especially young people. Volunteering provides opportunities to gain professional experience and to network while strengthening the local community. Volunteering offers numerous learning opportunities that empower us personally, develop our civic responsibility, and inspire us to practice excellence more and more.

MY PARENTS AS ROLE MODELS

When we want to be the best we can be, we don't stop until we finish, and we never give up. I lived by those parental values—those words were drilled into me. That kind of integrity was instilled in me as a child, and I carried it through my path in school and into my career. That kind of leadership is a gift we can bestow on our youth today. Our children are our legacy; it is imperative we be good role models.

What does it take to rise above mediocrity in a world that seems to be setting it as the new standard? People often want to get things done with little thought of the end result. The more "just getting things done" becomes the practice, the less the focus is on getting things right. After a while, "okay" becomes accepted and we no longer strive for excellence.

While listening to Joel Osteen speak about excellence, I realized how important my parents were as mentors to me. As Osteen described characteristics that develop the spirit of excellence, I pictured my parents and realized they were modeling excellence throughout the entire 20 years I lived with them. Their modeling was far more than setting high standards; they practiced excellence daily and I didn't realize it at the time. They encouraged my siblings and me to treat others as we want to be treated, to be on time, to dress properly, and to present ourselves in a way that we were proud of—because when you look good, you feel good, and you take care of your personal belongings and always keep the car, home, and office clean and tidy. These are practices my husband and I model for our children. We are providing them with tools to be the best they can be.

As a result, I was driven at a very young age. I needed excellence, and I was given the chance to express it. I was more than three decades into my career before I had enough pieces in place to feel I'd worked hard enough and had truly excelled. I was then ready to stop what I was good at doing in order to find the courage to utilize what I had learned, start again, and see if I had what it took to be successful on my own. It was difficult, but I knew I could do it, and that confidence remains with me still.

> Our children are our legacy; it is imperative we be good role models.

ENJOYING THE LANDSCAPE

I had been living a drive-by life since I graduated from college. In some ways I am still living that way, even after starting a new career. But now I look for the lessons in what I do, and examine every aspect of what I might have learned. For many years I did not do that. I just kept filling up, filling up, and filling up.

There were moments all along in my drive-by travels when I did pull over at a rest stop, get out of the car, and look around. When I was sending those bouquets and those cards and when I was holding the hands of my mother and my father as they lay dying—those were all among the stops along the journey.

And yet so often I also was fulfilling the expectations of others. Even though I loved the activity and thrived in it, it's only now I am really starting to see the bigger picture. I am grateful that along the way, my brother and sisters and I could see the importance of spending time with my parents. We were able to get a perspective on priorities.

Sometimes, until we slow down, we don't really realize what matters most in our life. It was only when I started reducing some of the baggage at work and the responsibilities as a project manager and started letting some things go that I would smile and begin to connect the dots. When we're running, we're not connecting the dots. In a lot of ways, I was in survival mode. I could have asked for help, I could have slowed down, but for some reason I had this need in me to do all those things. I have learned it's never too late to reconsider and change.

GIVING BACK AND FILLING UP

In the pursuit of excellence, giving back is what has filled me up. All the volunteer work, all the extra things I have done, and all of my service on those committees at work filled my heart and made me feel I was making a difference. I felt far more vibrant.

Those have been among the best of my experiences. I don't think I'll ever stop feeling that way. As my career takes a turn and moves on, I still hope to share my journey, and I still hope to make a difference in people's lives. I will always give back and promote the importance of contributing in that way.

Ask yourself: Are you lifting your life to your highest calling? You can select your path and maximize your potential. We have the power to change our communities to be better places to live for generations to come.

REACHING OUT

Sometimes people just need others to ask them to participate. They are waiting to give of themselves. They want to be invited, and then they will freely pursue excellence with a deep sense of commitment. It's a trickle effect: First comes a drop, then a trickle, and ultimately it can develop into a torrent. I have wondered at times why some people feel motivated to do more than others. Is it because we're not inviting those others to participate in the many available opportunities?

To be asked is very important. People want to give of themselves, but sometimes they need to be approached. It's an easy question— "Could you help me? Do you have a few minutes? Could I ask for your support?" Unless you ask, you can't expect an answer.

The journey of excellence is one of constant self-improvement, and I have been on that road for a long time, taking a close look at my own heart and looking within for flaws that may have led me to take on too much. I have come to recognize that excellence is more a matter of balance than of volume. That journey continues, as I actively and honestly look inside.

JOURNALING THE PROGRESS

Journaling is an important step in our pursuit of excellence. It helps us to measure our goals and to become more reflective. How can we hope to become our best without taking the time for self-reflection? It is so easy to criticize others, but it can be somewhat harder to look into ourselves critically—and yet that is what we must do.

When I first began to write down my thoughts, I struggled to find the time to do it, even though I set aside time on my calendar at the end of each day for that very purpose. One thing that slowed me down was my determination to get all of the words right. I found myself examining the grammar and the punctuation. I wanted perfection, but excellence of expression comes in more than the technicalities. I learned we don't have to be perfect when striving for excellence. Journaling became much easier and less frustrating once I started to blog. I began to write more naturally with whatever came to mind. I was able to take an ever-closer look at just who Linda Marshall is.

CONSIDER THIS:

Writing a journal doesn't have to be time consuming, and you don't have to be a writer. You start by committing five to ten minutes to write down some reflections on your day. Your journal doesn't have to be handwritten, but it needs to be held in a secure place for your eyes only. You may want to write about the following things:

- Daily events—work, family, leisure activities
- Personal thoughts and feelings about your life
- Travel experiences
- Future career goals
- Retirement dreams
- Bucket list

GIVING THE BEST OF OURSELVES

Every day, I try to take time to stop and be thankful for what I have and for those with whom I share my life. That's everything to me now. In my drive-by years, I did not do that as much as I should have. Looking back, I feel so sad for all the times I wasn't grateful. I'm finally digging into what it is I am grateful for and how it feels in the moment.

Life is a gift that we should cherish each day. Often, even now, I find my days so full of activity that I'm not practicing gratitude—and how can anyone be truly excellent without being grateful? Excellence is far more than doing well at tasks. We must appreciate others. We must be compassionate, accepting, and forgiving. Excellence may come from standing up for a principle, but I am also learning that it comes from knowing when to let things go.

One of the downfalls of being so passionate is that we can fall hard. When somebody disappoints us or when something hurts us, it can feel like a stab in the heart. It depletes our energy. A passionate soul rides the wave of excellence, but those highs can come crashing down. I struggle with this. I have found when I spend time examining myself I become far more observant in general. When people close to me are not practicing excellence, I notice it. It hurts to see those I love doing something I know they will regret.

> We have the power to change our communities to be better places to live for generations to come.

TAKING CARE OF YOU

Only you can take care of you. You know what your mind, body, and soul need in your pursuit of excellence. For many of us, our days are filled with many responsibilities, including caregiving for others, taking care of our homes, and working in and outside of our homes. If you take good care of yourself, you will be best prepared to take good care of others.

Your body is your temple, and you must nurture your mind, body, and spirit in order to be the best possible you. In my drive-by life, I focused on exercising and eating right, but I was missing the emotional element of my temple. You're not balanced unless you are looking at your life holistically, and I was not always doing that. It is so hard to keep your mind, body, and soul in balance. I am often missing one of those three, and I have to stop and revisit.

> Our performance is not enhanced when we are self-critical.

Self-compassion is taking care of you. We all make mistakes, and we must have the ability to review them with kindness and understanding. We need to learn to be gentle with ourselves. Our performance is not enhanced when we are self-critical. Practicing self-compassion can reduce stress and assist in positive movement forward.

To be the best you can be requires an attitude adjustment. It can be hard to do, but the spirit of excellence calls for it. I challenge myself regularly to question my choices, behaviors, and actions by asking, "Are these the best I can do?"

LETTING THE BRILLIANCE OUT

During speaking engagements and presentations, my emotions sometimes show. At one time, I tried hard to control that, but a lot of dear people have since convinced me to be comfortable showing my feelings. Showing how you feel isn't a weakness but rather a genuine expression that others can understand. I always get emotional when I talk about my parents or about other fine people who have moved on. I let audiences know in advance my voice may crack during a poignant story, and I might even need to stop. They just smile, and somehow it helps just knowing they understand.

In fact, even as I write these words I feel my eyes moistening, as has happened a number of times on this journey. To write a book is not easy, and I thank you, my readers, for coming along with me.

Excellence arises from the sharing of ourselves. We need to open ourselves to others—and it might only take a smile. After a recent workshop I conducted, an attendee came up to me. "You may recognize me from Mohawk," she said. "I passed you so many times in the hall and I'd see you smile. I never knew who you were, but thank you for those smiles."

Weeks later, when I was visiting the college to work on a project, I passed her again. This time, our exchange of smiles was brighter than ever, and we touched each other on the arm—a truly excellent moment. We had finally connected, with the only regret being that it hadn't happened sooner.

> In the words of Judy Garland, "Always be a first-rate version of yourself, instead of a second-rate version of somebody else."

How many times have you passed that person in the hallway, maybe with a nod, maybe with a quick smile, and never put a name to the face? How many times have you seen someone sitting alone and couldn't find a moment to chat? We need to make our connections. How can people know who we are unless we give them a chance to know?

> Everyone has the capacity to give, and we all give in different ways.

We all possess the attributes of strength, patience, and passion. Everyone has the capacity to give, and we all give in different ways. Each of us is a shining light. We need to find out where our passion lies, and then we need to let that brilliance out. Together, we can make this world such a bright place. Together, we can build toward excellence.

It has been said that there are three C's to excellence: courage, confidence, and contentment. When we have achieved excellence, we have the courage of our convictions, we have confidence in our decisions, and we are content we have done our best. Along the way, however, we need to indulge the habit of excellence, and in doing so we will come to know ourselves. In the words of Judy Garland, "Always be a first-rate version of yourself, instead of a second-rate version of somebody else."

RESPECT

CHAPTER FIVE

Have a big enough heart to love unconditionally, and a broad enough mind to embrace the differences that make each of us unique.
—D.B. Harrop

D o you practice the Golden Rule?

We all know the Golden Rule: we should treat people how we would want to be treated. The Platinum Rule is this: Treat people how they would want to be treated. It might not always be the best policy, but generally it's good to consider other people's needs and feelings.

One of the most important gifts we can share is the modeling of respectful behavior to those who surround us. We must set the bar high. Respect was a big part of my upbringing, and I struggle today as I observe the amount of disrespect in our society. I hear young people talking to their parents in a manner I would never have dreamed of using with my own parents.

"I've learned that people forget what you said, people forget what you did, but people never forget how you made them feel," said the late poet and author Maya Angelou. I know it to be true. That quote has been a game changer in my life and in the way I manage my business today. I forget sometimes what people say or who said it. I even forget, after a while, what people have done, because life's journey is long. But I never forget the impression of warmth that someone imparted. And if there was difficulty, the details might well escape the mind, yet the heart recalls the traces of the feelings. At a glimpse of that person's face, those impressions come back.

CONSIDER THIS:

Take a few minutes to review your day. Focus on one interaction with your supervisor or a colleague.

What do you remember most about the interaction?

Do you remember how the interaction made you feel?

Hopefully it was a positive interaction, because you will savor the memory forever—especially when you reconnect with that individual. Unfortunately, the same is true if it was a negative—you will likely remember how it felt for a long time.

CONTROLLING THE DISRESPECT

Respect allows others to be who they are. One adult should not orchestrate the course of another adult. Steve Gilliland discusses the disrespect of controlling behavior in *Hide Your Goat*.[11] I know I've practiced, unintentionally, such controlling behavior. To engage in positive and respectful relationships, he says, controlling behavior must be eliminated.

Sometimes, however, we don't realize we are doing it. That is why when somebody is upsetting or bothering you, the most respectful gift you can offer is to have the courage to tell that person in a kind way, "You know, when you say that, it really hurts me," or "I find that insulting," or "I find that to be disrespectful."

How else can you learn? Sometimes people don't have the courage to say that to those in positions of power. They should, or the disrespect is likely to continue, and it could even worsen. It takes practice to learn to speak up at the appropriate time, but it is necessary. It is actually a key part of giving back.

"I'm not concerned with your liking or disliking me," said Jackie Robinson, the first black player in the major leagues, as he told his white teammates on the Brooklyn Dodgers in 1947, "All I ask is that you respect me as a human being."

We should take those words to heart and put them into practice. On the job, for instance, we need not like every one of our colleagues. But we do have to respect them. It's healthy to disagree. We can kindly tell someone how we feel. But we cannot misbehave and disrupt the

> "I've learned that people forget what you said, people forget what you did, but people never forget how you made them feel."

workplace. That hurts everyone. It hurts the organization that hired us in good conscience to develop the mission, vision, and values of the organization, and therefore, it is your professional responsibility to act accordingly. It is not a choice.

"One of the most sincere forms of respect is actually listening to what another has to say," said author and speaker Bryant H. McGill.[12] We all have had the experience of talking to someone who makes little eye contact and seems to be rushing the conversation along, which can be very distracting as it detracts from sincere communication. Most of us have been guilty of that occasionally when in a hurry. But how does that make others feel? It comes across as rude and disrespectful. It is a symptom of a drive-by life.

Listening well has not always been easy for me on my journey. I'm becoming a better listener, but I have to work on it daily. I have a tendency to jump right in and share my thoughts, and I understand this is a behavior that arises from passion—but I have learned that listening to others is enriching. I am even more passionate and able to better relate when I sit tight and hear others out. For someone who has a lot of excitement and energy, that can be hard to do.

NO BULLIES ALLOWED

It has been said real power arises from self-respect, which leads to self-discipline. If you have gained control of your self-respect and your self-discipline, that's a step toward supreme excellence. If you lose respect for yourself, you can sink deeply and quickly. You may stop caring who you associate with. You may start associating with people who pull you even further down. This often happens to children. Could it be that the first step toward such unfortunate relationships later in life occurs when children feel that nobody is listening to them?

When children don't know the rules of engagement or the rules of respect, they can fall victim to bullies—or they can become bullies themselves. They haven't been taught those rules, or they have not seen enough modeling of respectful behavior. They reflect what they have seen or experienced. It's crucial adults practice respectful behavior because young people are watching. If we don't talk at home about respect and about agreeing to disagree, if we don't have those values as a foundation, then we are opening the door to bullying.

Among children, those who are doing the bullying have not learned those rules of engagement and respect. Generally they have low self-esteem, for whatever reason. Bullies don't feel good about themselves, and by putting other people down, they feel better. It's a power play often made worse by ignorance; they don't know how to behave, and they have not been conditioned to be so inclined.

It's also true the child who is being bullied needs to learn self-respect, so that he or she knows how to respond when someone is treating them poorly. Someone needs to tell them the basics—don't take it personally, and let the bully know that such behavior won't be accepted. If it continues, walk away from it and do what is necessary so that it is not repeated. It takes courage to confront a bully, and young people at such a tender age can find it hard to rally such courage. Their self-esteem is often still fragile. They are just not at that level of maturity. How do they gain it? By seeing it in action. By getting good advice. How do the grown-ups handle themselves? What do they have to say about such situations? Healthy discussions about topics such as this are so important.

Children also have to learn there is a difference between bullying and children's playful name calling. They need to be strong enough to take the occasional teasing. The key is learning to deal with it. They need to know when to ignore it and walk away, when to speak up for themselves without retaliating, and when it is time to ask an adult for help.

CONSIDER THIS:

Look around you. Is some child in need of your guidance?

Do you know any bullies who have graduated from the playground to the workplace? Often, the habit of disrespect endures.

How often do we act like children? Whether on the playground or in the workplace, bullying needs to be addressed appropriately.

People sometimes engage in power plays because they think they can get away with it. After all, they got away with it as children, and it worked for them. Nobody corrected that behavior. As adults, we need to take time to talk to children about right and wrong and about how to show respect. If we lack it in our own lives, it's high time we developed it, for our own sake and for the children's. If we don't do something to break that cycle, we are setting them up for a dysfunctional life.

RESPECTFUL CONFRONTATION

It's important not to confuse respect with avoiding conflict. If you don't raise the issue of disrespect and instead let it slip away in silence, you become part of the problem, whether you are dealing with a child or an adult. You're allowing and perpetuating disrespect by default. If you accept behavior, it will continue. That's a lesson I'm sure has been expressed to many people in family counseling, marriage counseling, and employee counseling. In so many situations of life, we need to remember that. You must tell people how you want to be treated. They need to know.

> "I'm not concerned with your liking or disliking me," said Jackie Robinson, the first black player in the major leagues, as he told his white teammates on the Brooklyn Dodgers in 1947, "All I ask is that you respect me as a human being."

All members of a team must act respectfully, without exception. A strong team will accept nothing less than a respectful work environment. A weak team promotes disrespect by allowing it. Find your voice and use it appropriately.

We all have our quirks. Not everyone's style will match yours. Some people are more forward in their interactions, and some are more circumspect. Sometimes we might find something irritating about someone's mannerisms or outlook, but that difference does not necessarily mean the person is being rude. Some people might grate on you simply because they are who they are, and because you are who you are. Accept them, as you would hope that they would accept you.

In deciding when to speak up, it can be a fine line, and that is why it is important to have a clear sense of boundaries. Know what you will accept and what you will not, and communicate that when necessary. Yes, we all are different, and part of respect is to accept those differences—while staying within the basic parameters of decency and civility.

LAUGHTER

CHAPTER SIX

The human race has one really effective weapon,
and that is laughter.
—Mark Twain

I s laughter a part of your daily life?

When I worked at Mohawk College, one of my daily joys was my morning smile ritual. Each morning I reached out to connect with anyone who crossed my path on the way to my office. Some were my colleagues and some were unknown to me. I smiled with my eyes, face, lips, and body. Opportunities to reach out were many, and it brought me such joy to see how people responded. It squeezed my heart and provided me with an abundance of energy, which carried me through my day. I received a dividend of delight, and I only had to invest a few smiles.

I continue that tradition to the best of my ability wherever I go, and feel so fortunate to receive that same squeeze in my heart. It is hard not to smile at someone who smiles at you. Simply reaching out and smiling at another human being creates a positive touch. Your smile holds the power to change the world, so don't let the world change your smile.

You have the power to build a positive world around you. If you are so fortunate as to wake up each morning, then you have the opportunity to make your day the best possible, for yourself and for those with whom you come in contact each and every day. Choose to be the best you can be, each and every day, as you create your living legacy.

A great way to begin is with smiles and laugher. They prime the soul to experience the joy that surrounds us—and joy is everywhere, if we are open to it. Laughter transcends cultures. "Everybody laughs the same in every language," the Ukrainian-born comedian Yakov Smirnoff observed, "because laughter is a universal connection."

> Your smile holds the power to change the world, so don't let the world change your smile.

When I went to Florida to visit my friend in the hospital, there was more than one occasion—when we were very worried and felt desperate about his condition—that the doctor told us we needed to bring some laughter into his recovery. And we did. We started telling stories and reminiscing with him. Even though my friend could not speak, he laughed loudly with his eyes while he held on tightly to our hands. The laughter and story-telling helped all of us to cope during a very serious situation.

In *The Joy Factor*, Susan Smith Jones[13] writes about how valuable it is to our souls to be able to laugh and to feel free to be silly. That can be a challenge for me sometimes, because I often have a serious, professional persona. I'm more likely to express such spontaneity when I am in my comfort zone, as I am sure is the case for many people.

When we let down our guard, our sense of humor blossoms. Some people seem hesitant to do that, but we need to remember that people want to see us laughing. They want to know who we really are and what makes us tick. We must express our humanity.

"Remember, laughter can be potent when things are looking gloomy," Smith says. If life is getting you down, you need a way to pick yourself up. We all have times in life when we need to draw on laughter and funny stories.

THE BEST MEDICINE

Laughter has been called the best medicine, and I do believe it's so. It's infectious, and people love the sound of it. It strengthens the immune system. It triggers healthy physical changes in the body. It boosts our energy, diminishes pain, and protects us from the damaging effects of stress.

Laughter is a gift that costs nothing.

Psychologist Paul McGhee, a researcher on humor and laughter, says, "Your sense of humor is one of the most powerful tools you have to make certain that your daily mood and emotional state support good health."[14] Employee morale has been consistently falling, he says, and the antidote is to make work fun. Fun and laughter reduce stress and negativity and ease the buildup of frustrations.

CONSIDER THIS:

When you feel in the grip of what seems to be a major problem, Paul McGhee suggests you ask yourself these questions:

Is it really worth getting upset over?

Is it worth upsetting others?

Is it that important?

Is it that bad?

Is the situation irreparable?

Is it really your problem?

If you don't have a sense of humor or you can't find that joy or that happy moment, you are going to struggle. You are going to have a hard time striving and reaching excellence. It's going to affect your work, and it's going to affect your personal life. It can even make it hard to get out of bed in the morning.

Laughter is a fundamental of good mental health. If you know someone who never seems to laugh, that person might be in need of some support. He or she might be struggling, and somebody close to them needs to reach out. It might not be you, but if you notice such heaviness of heart, you could suggest to someone else that a friendly word could work wonders.

Humor helps you keep a positive, optimistic outlook through difficult situations. It helps with disappointments and with loss. Have you ever been to a funeral visitation where people are telling stories about the deceased? Even though you lost that wonderful person in your life, it gives you great comfort to recall the fun times, the laughter, and the joy.

Laughter tends to come naturally when we are able to look on the bright side of things. But when you're in a state of sadness, you have to go far to find humor and laughter. In that case, you need to find things that are good in your life. And when you hear people laughing, move toward that precious sound. Don't hesitate to enter into the levity, saying, "Hey, what did I miss!?"

> Laughter has been called the best medicine, and I do believe it's so. It's infectious, and people love the sound of it. It strengthens the immune system. It triggers healthy physical changes in the body. It boosts our energy, diminishes pain, and protects us from the damaging effects of stress.

If you are living a life where there is often a smile on your face, pass it on. If you have enough joy in your heart to laugh with abandon, pass it on. You have been given the gift of humor. Share it. Someone else needs that medicine.

THE SOCIAL BENEFITS

You may have encountered people on the job who have a negative attitude. It's as if they were declaring, "I'm not going to laugh. I'm not happy. I don't want them to think I'm happy here." For those who feel that way, it's certainly time to find something new. If you can't find joy at work, if you can't feel free to have a hearty laugh or enjoy a moment of levity, then that's not a good environment for you. Humor and laughter are among the necessities of life.

People like being around happy people. Is it more likely or less likely that someone is going to approach you if you have a frown on your face? Whether you are looking for a job or for an item in the store, you will come across as far more approachable, and you will be more likely to get the help you need, if you adopt a positive, happy outlook.

I like to create experiences to have fun. I always try to come up with something different.

Sometimes life gets too serious. If you don't create the opportunities, then the good times won't happen. You have to be spontaneous.

When my daughters were teenagers, I wanted to spend more time with them while also doing something healthy. The solution was to take them to the gym with me. It turned out to be one of the best things we did together in their teenage years.

Although we had a lot of laughs at the gym, my daughters' main source of laughter was my attempts at yoga. The best way for me to learn is to be near the instructor, so I would usually get in the front row. My two girls would position themselves a few rows back, near the wall, where they had a great view of their mother trying her various yoga poses.

I became pure entertainment for them. Sometimes I would get stuck in a pose and probably looked like a fish caught in a net. The instructor would somehow manage to free me from my predicament as my daughters howled with laughter at my less than dignified maneuver. What did I learn from this lesson? Humility! I eventually decided yoga was best left for others to practice, but I cherish the memories.

LETTING THE LAUGHTER IN

I have recently found the joy of a pet—actually, it is my daughter's dog, Annie. My daughter and Annie recently lived with us for several months while they were waiting for their new home to be built. During their stay, I found great joy and many moments of mirth in Annie. She made me laugh and calmed me down when I felt anxious.

> Let the laughter into your life. You're a much more beautiful person when you're laughing and smiling. It attracts others to you. It opens your life to possibilities. It truly is a gift.

When my daughters were younger, I didn't allow them to have a dog because we were away from the house so often I thought we wouldn't be able to give a dog the love and attention it would deserve. After years of reflection, though, I understand it was more than that—I was fearful about how my daughters would feel when they lost their pets, as I remembered only too well how sad I felt when I lost my pets as a child. I didn't want them to have to feel that pain, but in the end, I also prevented them from the joy and laughter that a pet can give a child. With Annie, I was finally able to let a wonderful source of love and laughter return to my life.

Let the laughter into your life. You're a much more beautiful person when you're laughing and smiling. It attracts others to you. It opens your life to possibilities. It truly is a gift.

HEALTH BENEFITS OF LAUGHTER

In some of my workshops, I introduce laughter therapy to show how it can reduce stress and improve interpersonal skills. Researchers at the University of Michigan found that just 20 seconds of laughter can be as good for the lungs as three minutes on a rowing machine. The therapeutic effects of laughter have been studied clinically since the 1970s. There are now more than 5,000 laughter clubs worldwide.[15]

The goal of laughter therapy is to assist you to laugh with ease. It can be conducted in groups or individually. The process begins by introducing activities to get people to giggle. Oddly, fake laughter has the same results on the body as genuine laughter because our bodies are unable to distinguish between the two.

This activity can create exhaustion and elation at the same time. It reinforces the fact that we can laugh at any time, not just when we are happy, as our mood can be elevated through forced laughter. What I notice the most is how infectious laughter is. In some of my sessions, some individuals come close to losing control and have difficulty stopping the levity. It is very funny to observe a group when they are laughing together. It is sometimes challenging to settle the group down afterward, but it is very beneficial and works well.

CONSIDER THIS:

During a stressful period in your day, consider sharing a funny story or joke with your colleagues to reduce the tension and stressful atmosphere.

Some teams have a practice of sharing a joke or laugh before they begin the day.

Lee Berk and Stanley Tan at Loma Linda University studied the benefits of laughter and found it can improve health in a variety of ways. Among their findings:[16]

- It lowers blood pressure. It thereby reduces the risk of stroke and heart attack.

- It reduces the level of stress hormone, which may result in a stronger immune system.

- It tones the abdominal muscles.

- It improves cardiac health. A hearty laugh can burn as many calories as moderate exercise.

- It activates the immune system T cells to fight off sickness.

- It triggers the release of endorphins, the body's natural pain reliever.

- It enhances one's sense of well-being. Positivity has been shown to promote health.

Let the laughter back in. You're a much more beautiful person when you're laughing and smiling. It attracts others to you. It opens your life to possibilities. It truly is a gift that keeps on giving—to you and to others.

LEADERSHIP

CHAPTER SEVEN

The greatest leaders mobilize others by coalescing
people around a shared vision.
—Ken Blanchard

What kind of leader are you?

What kind of leader would you like to be?

"A leader is like a shepherd," Nelson Mandela wrote in his 1994 autobiography, *Long Walk to Freedom*. "He stays behind the flock, but the most nimble go out ahead, whereupon the others follow, not realizing that all along they are being directed from behind."[17]

Mandela's words speak to the need for a shift in power. Sometimes leaders feel they have to have all the power and control. By contrast, the type of leader who herds those in the flock, who pushes them in the right direction—who leads from behind—is one who operates without ego and from a position of true strength.

During my career, I always tried to find the strengths in others and keep my own ego in check. I certainly was not perfect. But as a role model and as a leader, it's okay to make mistakes—as long as you can at least acknowledge you have made them and say your apologies.

Tom Osborne, in his book *Tom Osborne on Leadership: Life Lessons from a Three-Time National Championship Coach*, writes about one of his principles, "Be a servant leader. Sacrifice yourself for the benefit of others."[18] I subscribe to that. I feel that in many situations, a servant leader is one of the best types you can be.

To be a servant leader, you have to know yourself. You need the quality of self-reflection. You also must have a desire to serve others and a commitment to lead. You cannot just jump in and then change your mind. You have to be trustworthy, self-aware, and very humble.

Humility is essential in leadership. If you don't have that, you may come across as being arrogant. People want to support leaders in whom they believe and to whom they relate. They want someone they can trust. Arrogance doesn't have a role in that, and yet sometimes leaders get to a point where they feel they are above relating to people. There's a problem there. A leader must be caring as well as visionary. A good leader believes in the value of relationships.

Leadership has many styles, and at various times and in various situations, some styles of leadership are more effective than others. If you start out as a servant leader, however, I believe you will gain and keep the respect of the people you are leading, even if you have to switch to a different style to be more effective.

> Humility is essential in leadership.

Leadership must be built on respect. A thoughtful leader gains trust by showing he or she knows the goals of the team and has been faithful to them in the past. Even if there is disagreement on the course of action, the team should understand that some compelling reason is behind it, and there is merit in agreeing to disagree. Negativity will derail the mission.

A leader needs to establish these things up front and say, "I have your back. I'm going to be there for you, but I need you to be there for me." It goes both ways.

The book *Winning* by Jack Welch includes the following list of "What Leaders Do":[19]

1. Leaders relentlessly upgrade their team, using every encounter as an opportunity to evaluate, coach, and build self-confidence.

2. Leaders make sure people not only see the vision, they live and breathe it.

3. Leaders get into everyone's skin, exuding positive energy and optimism.

4. Leaders establish trust with candor, transparency, and credit.

5. Leaders have the courage to make unpopular decisions and gut calls.

6. Leaders probe and push with a curiosity that borders on skepticism, making sure their questions are answered with action.

7. Leaders inspire risk taking and learning by setting the example.

8. Leaders celebrate.

CONSIDER THIS:

Think back to leaders you highly respect and those you do not. List the top ten actions you have observed that inspire you.

1. _____

2. _____

3. _____

4. _____

5. _____

6. _____

7. _____

8. _____

9. _____

10. _____

THE PARADE OF PRESIDENTS

Over the course of my career at Mohawk College, I was fortunate to learn firsthand about leadership by observing the many different presidents who led the college during mostly five-year terms. Each time, this leadership change led to enormous change and transition for the entire organization.

Because of the type of work I did at the college, I had the opportunity to work with many of the presidents. We had strong leaders with very different strengths, which undoubtedly helped to propel the college to new heights. It was inspiring to observe and listen to them. I am grateful to have learned a great deal about leadership qualities while on the job.

Each leader brought a vision and expertise, which led to an array of opportunities for the organization and the community. Most often I agreed with the direction they took, but when I didn't agree, I accepted their position and respected the process. Even the opportunity to participate in a process you don't necessarily agree with can profoundly influence your holistic understanding of leadership. Don't let these opportunities go to waste. Be present in the activity, and learn from it.

FOR THE STRENGTH OF THE TEAM

I like to lead, and I have filled that role many times in my work and volunteer life. It is my nature. But I can be a great team player, too. A good leader needs a strong team. One does not always need to be the person in charge. You can fill essential roles as a member of the board or as a player on the team. I have served fulfilling roles both as a board officer and as a board member.

You should avoid stepping into a leadership role until you are ready. You need to take the time to learn about the organization and to plan thoughtfully. When you are passionate and excited about the responsibility you have been given, sometimes you want to do it all right away. But it's often better to sit back and observe.

Unfortunately, there are times when people are put in positions before they are ready to lead and times when people are considered leaders when there are actually playing a management role. There is a difference between management and leadership. Peter F. Drucker states, "Management is doing things right; leadership is doing the right things."[20]

Robert Locke describes this distinction well in his article, "7 Ways to Tell the Difference Between Real Leadership and Good Management," where he describes the roles and responsibilities of leaders:[21]

- A manager deals with tasks while a leader develops relationships.

- A manager will rarely think outside the box while a leader will engineer change.

- A leader seeks to empower while a manager looks to micromanage.

- A manager will maintain systems while a leader will inspire followers.

- A leader will use emotional intelligence while a manager may be less aware.

- A leader will exploit opportunities while a manager avoids risk.

- A leader needs much more charisma than a manager.

EMOTIONAL INTELLIGENCE AND LEADERSHIP

Over the course of my career, I've observed many leadership styles, and after spending considerable time researching leadership and leader behaviors, I've come to realize how important strong emotional intelligence is to effective leadership.

In the early 1990s, psychology professors John D. Mayer and Peter Salovey coined the term "emotional intelligence", with Mayer defining it as "the ability to accurately perceive your own and others' emotions," with the additional ability "to understand the signals that emotions send about relationships," plus manage those emotions, including your own. By the late 1990s, Rutgers psychologist Daniel Goleman applied it to the business world.

"The most effective leaders are all alike in one crucial way," writes Goleman in a Harvard Business Review article. "They all have a high degree of what has come to be known as emotional intelligence."[22] Like Goleman, I've come to understand that a good IQ and strong technical skills matter for entry-level executives, but to be a great leader it takes more than "an incisive, analytical mind, and an endless supply of smart ideas."

More interesting is the knowledge that emotional intelligence can be learned. Many believe reducing stress, remaining focused, and staying connected to yourself and others will help you increase your emotional intelligence. This can be achieved by practicing activities like meditation, reflection, and relaxation, all of which can increase those interpersonal skills that make working with people easier. Being mindful of situations and learning to appreciate how the other person is feeling can go a long way toward positively affecting your emotional intelligence.

> "The most effective leaders are all alike in one crucial way,"
>
> "They all have a high degree of what has come to be known as emotional intelligence."

Like most people I am not at my best when I am in a stressful situation. I have learned over time that if I don't practice mindfulness and remain focused, I am unable to leverage or further develop my emotional intelligence skills, which have a significant impact on how I lead.

We've all witnessed local, national, and international leaders who seem to have a good sense of the people around them and others who definitely lack the ability to empathize and/or sympathize. And regardless of the type of leadership style you practice, certainly strong "people skills" are key to being a successful leader.[23]

LEADERS READ BOOKS

In his article "25 Books That Will Teach the Most Powerful Leadership Lessons," Dean Bokhari shares that among the leaders that he has interviewed, most state that they read books regularly. Bokhari says, "Books are like training weights for the brain." A few of my favorites on his list are:[24]

- *Primal Leadership* by Daniel Goleman
- *The Seasons of Life* by Jim Rohn
- *Emotional Intelligence 2.0* by Travis Bradberry
- *The 7 Habits of Highly Effective People* by Stephen Covey
- *The Effective Executive* by Peter F. Drucker
- *Start With Why* by Simon Sinek

Clearly no one leadership style works in all situations. As mentioned previously, leadership has many styles, and at various times and in various situations, some styles are more effective than others. Effective leaders are able to practice the best approach as the need arises.

RELATIONSHIPS

CHAPTER EIGHT

Trust is the glue of life. It's the most essential ingredient in effective communication. It's the foundational principle that holds all relationships.
—Stephen Covey

How healthy are your work and personal relationships? When I conduct speaking and teaching engagements on the "Journey to Excellence," I ask participants, "Would you like to be the best you can be, work at the highest functioning level, and influence others?" Most people want to be the best they can be; however, understanding what that means and practicing it is not as easy as it sounds.

When facilitating my Personality Dimensions®/True Colors® workshops, I am often surprised by how coworkers react when they learn how little they really know about each other. Colleagues who have worked together for years often don't really know the person sitting next to them. When individuals do their self-assessments, they have a better understanding of their own personality and how to work with people of the four personality types. Knowing our own dominant personality temperament assists in understanding our personal strengths and biases while learning to appreciate and accept the differences in others.

Personality Dimensions, a trademarked human relations tool based on leading edge research in human motivation and behavior, takes a close look at personality types, the expectations that people set, and how they get along. It helps to explain what motivates behavior in people with different temperaments.

Personality Dimensions is based on the work of Carl Jung, David Keirsey, and Linda Berens and draws on a long history of knowledge about human temperament. The workshops I conduct are interactive, with a self-discovery format. Going through this workshop enhances people's self-esteem, dignity, self-worth, and relationships with family, friends, and colleagues.

When I conduct workshops or seminars in organizations, the people often see, of course, that they represent a range of personalities. I explain they can use that human variety to their benefit—they can put the differences to work for the betterment of their lives and the organizations that they work for. Relationships are an

> Knowing our own dominant personality temperament assists in understanding our personal strengths and biases while learning to appreciate and accept the differences in others.

extremely important part of a person's life, so it is critical that we focus on developing healthy relationships.

TAKING THE HIGH ROAD

Today, I choose the higher road—the path of charity, acceptance, love, selflessness, kindness.
—Jonathan Lockwood Huie

In my life, there are times when taking the high road is an unbearable act. The hardest challenge occurs when I'm involved in a disagreement regarding a principled matter. I know in my heart I am right, and I have the need to state my truth. Actually, at times, I want to shout it out loud to let it be known that I am right. Sometimes I have done just that.

I'm sure I have been overbearing and bullish. When that happens, I regret my behavior and am ashamed and disappointed in myself. The disappointment can linger for days and months afterward. At such times when I let my ego take over, I clearly am not striving for excellence or attempting to be the best I can be.

There is something to be said about "agreeing to disagree." This is a respectful way for all involved to have their say. Truly, it shouldn't matter if all parties agree, unless of course it is a life-threatening situation. Taking the high road is not easy when listening to someone who is obnoxious, insulting, and perhaps bullying, but it is truly rewarding when we can walk away without raising our voice or losing patience. When we take the high road, we have our integrity intact. I can live happily with that.

CULTIVATING THE CONNECTIONS

As I have mentioned, I truly am a relationship person. I try to let people know how I feel, but again, it's how we make other people feel that's so important. I care about the people in my life, whether it's a family member or my hair stylist. I find ways to demonstrate how much they mean to me. I feel it is important to show my gratitude that they are in my life.

Relationships are central in our lives. Throughout the day, we have relationships of varying degrees with so many people—from the mail deliverer, to the coffee shop attendant, to our coworkers, to friends and family.

CONSIDER THIS:

How do you treat the people in your life?

Do you take time to speak to them?

Do you share your appreciation for their contribution to your work projects?

Do you find ways to support them if needed?

Do you take them for granted?

THE RULES OF ENGAGEMENT

My expectations are high, so I want you to treat me the way anybody would want to be treated. For the sake of the relationship, that expectation must not unravel. To that end, we have to set healthy rules—what I call rules of engagement—and everybody has to follow them in order to have a cooperative relationship. When we don't follow those rules, we have to be able to say, "I'm sorry, I made a mistake." Most of the time it has been in my home life when I have had to say this. Families tend to love us unconditionally, and when we know that—when we know they will love us no matter what—we sometimes let down our guard and act out. I can be quite direct. I'm not hurtful, but that directness can hurt feelings. I have had to apologize at times and explain that I didn't mean to come across the way I did or that I only raised my voice because I wasn't sure I could be heard. I apologize or clarify.

> When you take the time to fix mistakes, moving forward is possible, and it's likely you won't make the same mistakes twice.

If we cannot say we're sorry when we make a mistake, we are going to have issues. We own our mistakes, and therefore, we have to correct our errors. Otherwise, our relationships will suffer. Our relationships should be open and healthy enough so that people feel free to call us out on our behavior and we feel free to make amends. The best way to do that is face-to-face. My experience is that the sooner we repair the damages, the sooner we can move on. Waiting prolongs the negatives within and around us because issues don't repair themselves. When you take the time to fix mistakes, moving forward is possible, and it's likely you won't make the same mistakes twice.

FINDING COURAGE TOGETHER

So many times in my life, there have been people who were the wind beneath my wings, and I try hard to be the wind beneath other people's wings. We can't always be the bird soaring. We need to have people lifting us up, but we must be willing to lift other people up. When we build a relationship, each party gains support and power from the other.

I leaned on my relationships with a number of people before deciding to change directions and launch Marshall Connects. It was wonderful to trust others—to be able to reach out for support and to know those individuals were looking out for my best interest. Having a strong relationship with somebody we respect and who has something to share helps give us courage.

We build strength when we have experts that we trust and can reach out to. We can't possibly know everything, but it is truly a gift when we know where our resources are. That is true empowerment.

Having strong networks strengthens us as professionals and improves our relationships with others. Networking expands our general knowledge, keeps us current in our field, provides us with expert contacts, expands career opportunities, and allows us to give back to others.

CONSIDER THIS:

How strong is your professional network?

Do you use social media to:

- communicate your accomplishments?

- keep in contact with past and current contacts?

- build new connections?

Have you joined any professional associations?

Do you make it your practice to follow up with all new contacts?

Do you strategize on your networking approach before you attend a meeting or event?

Do you actively engage prospective contacts throughout events?

Be open to opportunities. Information can be powerful if you are open to listening. When I was growing up, many times my father would share his opinions, and honestly I didn't always want to listen, but I remember him saying, "What I share with you is a gift; you may keep or let it go."

I had felt secure and safe in my long-term career where people seemed like family, but I was ready to move on. As I moved on to my new career, I built relationships with people I trusted and respected. They were all instrumental in helping me transition into my new life; they had so much information and experience. These people were the wind beneath my wings, and I will be forever grateful.

I feel confident I am on the right path and have made good decisions. I know there will be bumps in the road—but I'm going in the right direction, and that's the great thing about building relationships with people we trust. We have to find people who will live up to our standards and can help in areas where we might need some support. Once we build those relationships, we can open ourselves up to further possibilities in our lives.

Again, it takes courage, but it can make us so much stronger. Sometimes we don't think we need help or a change. But again, when people ask for help and they get it, they become even stronger. I had to be willing to accept it. I had to ask for it, and I had to be willing to receive it, and that's when I really found my strength.

THE SANCTITY OF TRUST

Sometimes, as I said before, there are times when we have to distance ourselves from people who are simply not working anymore. Relationships change when we find our values do not align, and if that happens, we can no longer be in that relationship. It is unhealthy to stay, but it may take some time to plan the appropriate exit from a dysfunctional relationship.

I think of my father's words, "Your trust is your bond, and if you break trust you lose a great deal. That's all you have, and once you break that, you have nothing with that person." It's very hard to regain trust. You have to be true to people. Even after the apologies, once trust is broken, there will be an air of expectation—of caution.

In the workplace, building strong relationships is vital. People give to people they know and trust. Once they develop trust, they are willing to share their time and resources. If you are not a trustworthy person, or if you break someone's trust, you do indeed lose a great deal.

This happens so many times to charities when people lose their trust in them. There are many other ways to give back, and people who are charitably inclined can easily find another venue to support. If your public image is soiled or if you change your mission inexplicably, you will lose donors—you will lose their trust, their allegiance, and their

> "Your trust is your bond, and if you break trust you lose a great deal.

loyalty. It happens in relationships big and small, personal and corporate.

When people give back, they do so out of a sense of trust. They trust a person, an entity, or a cause with their money, and in turn, we trust that our time and efforts are valued and respected. It is a sacred relationship, and like all others that we care about, it must never be taken lightly.

Our integrity and ability to be trusted consistently in everything we do will provide the strong foundation of healthy, long-lasting work and personal relationships.

LEGACY

CHAPTER NINE

Legacy is not what's left tomorrow when you're gone.
It's what you give, create, impact and contribute today
while you're here that then happens to live on.
—Rasheed Ogunlaru

What does legacy mean to you?

Have you considered what your legacy will be?

To many people, "legacy" means what we leave as a gift or endowment, but it goes far beyond that. Your legacy involves much more than the amount of money or property you leave. It is very personal and distinctly individual.

When participating in a legacy exercise with my career coach, I began to really understand what legacy meant to me. I learned our legacy is much more than what people say about us after we die. Our legacy is what they say about us when we're alive, when we walk by their office, when we walk down the hall. Our legacy is defined by our actions, not our words. That's our living legacy.

> Who we really are is defined by what we do when we think no one is watching us.

While we're here on this earth, we're creating our legacy every day of our lives. Legacy is a lasting impression that we leave, as a result of everything we do each day. It's tied very closely to our integrity; who we really are is defined by what we do when we think no one is watching us. As the comedian Joe E. Lewis quipped, "You only live once, but if you work it right, once is enough."

Will you be deliberate about the legacy you're creating while you're alive so you can enjoy it while you are on earth? Many individuals are adopting the practice of giving while they are still here to see the impact. They gain the satisfaction of seeing how they have helped to make a difference.

THE SOWING OF MEMORIES

You can give to a charity or an esteemed cause, or you can simply do something thoughtful for your family members that will live on in their memories.

Years ago, my parents created a memorable experience for me, my siblings, and our partners. They planned a special dinner, ending it with a drive to a building that had four vehicles inside—one for each of us, with colors we had chosen unknowingly a few months earlier. It was an awesome surprise and one that we all relive from time to time.

My parents did things like that. "We want to see you enjoy your life," they would say. "We want to see how you manage the gifts we give you while we're alive." They wanted to enjoy these experiences. As a matter of fact, I can still close my eyes and see the joy on my parents' faces and the utterly surprised faces and squeals of delight from my family members—I still feel the excitement 20 years later.

We will all remember that day forever. At my parents' funerals, one of my siblings mentioned that day and that unexpected and thoughtful gift from our wonderful parents. That's part of what legacy is all about. They didn't leave us a car—they left us a treasured memory.

CONSIDER THIS:

Think about your life and consider all of the people, places, and things that bring you joy.

What makes you stop and smile?

Are there things that you do for others that will create a smile when a memory slips into their mind?

Have you considered developing opportunities to create memories for yourself and others?

What memory treasures can you give to others?

WHEN OUR LOVED ONES LEAVE

A few years ago, my brother-in-law, my older sister's husband, died suddenly in his sleep. He was only 54 years old.

He left a legacy for his children and family, but his sudden departure shook everyone. Since his passing we think of him often and miss him, and at the same time, many of us have reexamined our lives. Death can happen so easily. A heart attack, a car accident—there are no guarantees we will have a tomorrow with those we love. We need to embrace excellence while we are here.

I return to a theme that plays like a refrain in my life—in all our lives. When the people who loved us and whom we loved are gone, they take a piece of us with them. Then we are left here to build upon what is left, to be our very best so that those who are no longer with us here would be proud of us.

How do you want to be remembered? What do you want people to think of you—not just at the end of your life but at the end of today? What view of you will they take away from your next conversation?

"Language allows us to reach out to people, to touch them with our innermost fears, hopes, disappointments, victories," author Simon Van Booy wrote, "To reach out to people we'll never meet. It's the greatest legacy you could ever leave your children or your loved ones: the history of how you felt."

OUR CHILDREN, OUR LEGACY

One of Billy Graham's famous quotes is "The greatest legacy one can pass on to one's children and grandchildren is not money or other material things accumulated in one's life, but rather a legacy of character and faith." Recently when I chatted with my eldest daughter about what legacy meant to her, she shared that this was her favorite quote and that she had posted it in her office at work. I was so touched and so proud to hear that.

A poem that my siblings and I found recently while pulling together our father's ninth memoriam for the newspaper was so meaningful to all of us and reminded us of our parents.

Our parents kept a garden.
A garden of the heart;
They planted all the good things,
That gave all of us our start.
They turned us to the sunshine,
And encouraged us to dream:
Fostering and nurturing
The seeds of self-esteem.
And when the winds and rain came,
They protected us enough;
But not too much because they knew
We would stand up strong and tough.
Their constant good example,
Always taught us right from wrong;
Markers for our pathway
That will last a lifetime long.
We are our parents' garden,
We are their legacy.

—anonymous[25]

LEADERS COME AND LEADERS GO

Over the years I have had the pleasure of supporting numerous organizations as a volunteer and philanthropist, and as I have mentioned, all of these experiences played a role in shaping who I am today. To be honest, some of my experiences have been challenging and at times disappointing, but nevertheless, each held an opportunity for growth. I have come to realize that not all people placed in leadership roles have the necessary background or depth of community experience to lead. It pains me to realize the motives of individuals who are there not to enhance the organization but to advance their own agendas. An important lesson I learned is that people should not hold an organization responsible for leaders who disappointed them or the community. It is neither fair nor appropriate to do so.

In most cases we are drawn to organizations for a purpose, be it personal or professional; therefore, our relationship is always with the organization. We are responsible for challenging and questioning leadership not living up to the organizations' missions, visions, and values. That is our fundamental fiduciary responsibility as a board and community member. We are charged with stating our truths and the facts as we know them. When all is said and done, we may have to step back, take a break, and create some distance and time away.

I struggle when I have to step away from an organization because I become part of the organization as a volunteer, and it becomes part of me. Since passion is involved, it really hurts to walk away, but I am learning that we must always keep the organization and our initial intention in mind.

GIVING TRAIL BLAZER

In 2006, Warren Buffett, an amazing philanthropist and role model, pledged 99 percent of his estate to charity during his lifetime or at his death. He states, "The reaction of my family and me to our extraordinary good fortune is not guilt, but rather gratitude. Were we to use more than 1 percent of my claim checks on ourselves, neither our happiness nor our well-being would be enhanced. In contrast, that remaining 99 percent can have a huge effect on the health and welfare of others. That reality sets an obvious course for me and my family: keep all we can conceivably need and distribute the rest to society, for its needs. My pledge starts us down that course."[26]

THE GIFT OF YOU

When you give back, you are giving back of yourself. In many ways you are giving back the values that others gave to you. You are passing them on. Generations hence, someone will be better off because of who you were and what you chose to do.

Each of us is a small piece of a very big picture, and we should strive to present the best of humanity. We need to project that. That's what we're passing on. Sure, we can pass on money, and we can pass on an estate. But money and property are simply reflections of what we gained in life. Certainly if you have money to pass on, you are giving of yourself. The money represents your best efforts.

It's that old familiar question: why must it take losing someone or something for us to realize what we had? It's part of the drive-by phenomenon. It was after my parents' passing I truly felt the meaning of all they had done for us—and that in turn led me to reflect on my own legacy. It's a theme I am revisiting in this book, chapter after chapter—and that is because so many of these matters of the heart are intertwined. In

> When you give back, you are giving back of yourself. In many ways you are giving back the values that others gave to you.

one way or another, all of them are tied into relating well with others, appreciating what we have, and giving back of yourself.

WRITING MY LEGACY

When I began to create my legacy, I had to find a period of personal time where I could sit quietly and reflect on all of the aspects of my life. I considered the individuals I interacted with each day and was amazed at how many there were. I then reflected on the type of relationship that I had with each of them, which led me to understand the importance of all of the people in my life. So many people and organizations have played a significant role in my life, and I was beginning to see how much they have all meant to me. Gratitude plays a big role in my legacy, as I believe it does for others.

I began an exercise that my career coach gave me, and it was quite challenging. Basically I had to visualize myself sitting through an event where people from my personal and professional life would be celebrating my life's accomplishments. They would speak of how I supported them and made a positive difference, and they would speak of my character.

My next step in the exercise was to write down what I believe a specific family member, a friend, and a work and volunteer colleague would say about my contributions, character, and achievements. That was really difficult. I knew what I wanted them to say, but I wondered what they would actually say given the opportunity. The exercise felt a bit like eavesdropping on the eulogy at my own funeral. It was quite a strange feeling and yet very empowering in so many ways. It encouraged me to consider what I have to give and what my real strengths are. It provided me with a list of items that I need and want to work on for my living legacy.

CONSIDER THIS:

Living Legacy Exercise

Schedule in a time to sit quietly and reflect on the following questions:

Who do you interact with on a daily basis?

How important is your relationship with these individuals?

If asked, what would your family, friends, and colleagues say about your contributions to their lives?

What would they say about your life achievements to date?

What would they say about your character?

Reading Jan Johnston Osburn's article "Time to Write a New Chapter in Your Life? Five Ways to Get You Started" really inspired me. She states, "Until the final sentence has been written, there's still time to change the story... It doesn't matter what chapter or phase of the book you're currently in because each day presents another opportunity to write something new. It's up to you. This is your life and career legacy. Write your story the way you want to live it."[27]

It's all about the laughter, the respect, the optimism, and the gratitude and joy. It's all about the people with whom we share the journey. What will be the legacy that we leave behind in the hearts of others? All of this is what makes us; it can take us to our very best. This is excellence.

EPILOGUE

JOYFUL GIVING

Remember when you leave this earth, you can take with you nothing that you have received; only what you have given: a heart enriched by honest service, love, sacrifice, and courage.

—St. Francis of Assisi

A heart full of gratitude is a heart that gives. When we're grateful we have a desire to give back, and in giving back, we find joy. We get because we give.

Nothing material lasts. What endures are the relationships, the experiences, and the love. These are forever—the gifts that keep giving. Life is better when we are happy but even better when others are happy because of us.

Each chapter of this book is about one aspect in the journey of life. Together, these aspects become an irrepressible force that should compel us to give back to the best of our ability. They add up to a culture of caring that can permeate our lives—in our families, in our workplaces, and in all our dealings with others along the way.

Joyful giving will be an ongoing part of my journey; that I know for sure.

THINGS I HAVE LEARNED ALONG THE WAY:

- Lifelong learning is essential to my personal growth.
- I am always accountable for my behavior and actions without excuse.
- Each day is a new day where I can begin with a fresh start.
- Creating to-do lists and maintaining them daily supports my goal achievement.
- As a parent, I am responsible for modeling and teaching the necessary leadership skills to my children to reach out and make the world a better place.
- I can model emotional intelligence to my family, friends, and peers by how I choose to react and respond to their emotions.
- Mediocrity can't be tolerated on a journey to excellence.
- Taking care of mind, body, and soul is essential to practicing excellence.
- It is not possible for everyone to like me.
- I don't have to like everyone I interact with, but I will conduct myself respectfully with them.

- Reading provides a great source of knowledge and inspiration.

- Hard physical work is very fulfilling and motivating.

- Nature's beauty is one of God's greatest gifts.

- Problems are only solved with solutions.

- Family must be a priority to live a balanced life.

- Surrounding myself with like-minded people will support me on my journey to excellence.

- I must manage my habits so they are positive and support my goals.

- Fitting in is not a requirement.

- There is a huge difference between want and need, and knowing the difference is key.

- If I don't believe in myself, no one else will.

- I need to accept the things that I cannot change.

- Giving up is not an option.

- Asking for help is a sign of strength.

- Building relationships is essential to forward movement.

- Practicing gratitude daily is essential to sustain your life.

- Passion is essential to personal and professional growth.

- Respect is earned.

- Being authentic to oneself and others is necessary to preserve reputation and character.

NOTES FROM CHAPTER 1: JOY

CHAPTER 1 – JOY
"CONSIDER THIS" EXERCISES

i. Are you where you want to be today?

_____

What are your plans for tomorrow?

_____

If you were given an opportunity to make a change at work, what would it be?

_____

If you were given an opportunity to make a change in your personal life, what would it be?

_____

Where is your next destination in your journey of life?

_____

ii. Think of the colleagues you work with. Is there an individual or a small group you may be able to reach out to and brighten their day?

_____

You may want to start by doing something for one person or for everyone if it's a small group. What you do could be as simple as bringing in a special something to eat. Observe the response.

NOTES FROM CHAPTER 2: GRATITUDE

CHAPTER 2 – GRATITUDE "CONSIDER THIS" EXERCISES

i. Each morning, set your alarm to wake you up 15 minutes earlier than you need to, to allow yourself time to practice gratitude and to focus on the positive aspects of your previous day, week, and life in general. This may be the best 15 minutes of your day. Ensure you take time to fine-tune the rest of your waking hours.

ii. Give yourself the "Gratitude Reality Check." Send a quick email to ten friends or relatives and ask these questions:

- What work benefits do you receive?

_____

- What is the financial value of those benefits?

_____

The responses may surprise you. You may find many people won't be able to answer these questions in full. Upon investigating, they might be surprised to see what they actually receive in benefits. Sometimes we go to work each day and become part of a routine that doesn't allow us to stop and consider our surroundings. Our pay cheques are deposited into our bank accounts, and most, if not all, the money is already spent to pay our bills. Unless we lose our jobs or become ill, we often take for granted the benefits of our employment.

NOTES FROM CHAPTER 3: OPTIMISM

CHAPTER 3 – OPTIMISM
"CONSIDER THIS" EXERCISES

i. What brought you joy when you were young?

_____

_____

What made you happy then?

_____

_____

What made you happy a few months or a year ago, when things were really good in your life?

_____

_____

Get back in touch with what motivated you then.

Consider today's possibilities and opportunities, and begin to dream again.

NOTES FROM CHAPTER 4: EXCELLENCE

CHAPTER 4 – EXCELLENCE
"CONSIDER THIS" EXERCISES

i. Ask yourself the questions below to assess your journey to excellence:
- Are you passionate about being excellent?
- Do you have an inspiring goal?
- Have you developed a realistic strategy?
- Do you have a mentor?
- Are you a lifelong learner?
- Are you resilient?
- Will you continue to the end without giving up?
- Will you ask others for support along the way?
- Are you willing to work both smart and hard?

ii. Writing a journal doesn't have to be time consuming, and you don't have to be a writer. You start by committing five to ten minutes to write down some reflections on your day. Your journal doesn't have to be handwritten, but it needs to be held in a secure place for your eyes only. You may want to write about the following things:

- Daily events—work, family, leisure activities
- Personal thoughts and feelings about your life
- Travel experiences
- Future career goals
- Retirement dreams
- Bucket list

NOTES FROM CHAPTER 5: RESPECT

CHAPTER 5 – RESPECT
"CONSIDER THIS" EXERCISES

i. Take a few minutes to review your day. Focus on one interaction with your supervisor or a colleague.

What do you remember most about the interaction?

_____

Do you remember how the interaction made you feel?

_____

Hopefully it was a positive interaction, because you will savor the memory forever—especially when you reconnect with that individual. Unfortunately, the same is true if it was a negative—you will likely remember how it felt for a long time.

ii. Look around you. Is some child in need of your guidance?

Do you know any bullies who have graduated from the playground to the workplace? Often, the habit of disrespect endures.

How often do we act like children? Whether on the playground or in the workplace, bullying needs to be addressed appropriately.

NOTES FROM CHAPTER 6: LAUGHTER

CHAPTER 6 – LAUGHTER
"CONSIDER THIS" EXERCISES

i. When you feel in the grip of what seems to be a major problem, Paul McGhee suggests you ask yourself these questions:

> *Is it really worth getting upset over?*
> *Is it worth upsetting others?*
> *Is it that important?*
> *Is it that bad?*
> *Is the situation irreparable?*
> *Is it really your problem?*

ii. During a stressful period in your day, consider sharing a funny story or joke with your colleagues to reduce the tension and stressful atmosphere.

Some teams have a practice of sharing a joke or laugh before they begin the day.

NOTES FROM CHAPTER 7: LEADERSHIP

CHAPTER 7 – LEADERSHIP
"CONSIDER THIS" EXERCISES

i. Think back to leaders you highly respect and those you do not. List the top ten actions you have observed that inspire you.

1. _____

2. _____

3. _____

4. _____

5. _____

6. _____

7. _____

8. _____

9. _____

10. _____

NOTES FROM CHAPTER 8: RELATIONSHIPS

_____

_____

_____

_____

_____

_____

_____

_____

_____

_____

_____

_____

_____

_____

_____

_____

CHAPTER 8 – RELATIONSHIPS
"CONSIDER THIS" EXERCISES

i. How do you treat the people in your life?

_____

Do you take time to speak to them?

_____

Do you share your appreciation for their contribution to your work projects?

_____

Do you find ways to support them if needed?

_____

Do you take them for granted?

_____

ii. How strong is your professional network?

_____

Do you use social media to:
- communicate your accomplishments?
- keep in contact with past and current contacts?
- build new connections?

_____

Have you joined any professional associations?

_____

Do you make it your practice to follow up with all new contacts?

_____

Do you strategize on your networking approach before you attend a meeting or event?

_____

Do you actively engage prospective contacts throughout events?

_____

NOTES FROM CHAPTER 9: LEGACY

CHAPTER 9 – LEGACY
"CONSIDER THIS" EXERCISES

i. Think about your life and consider all of the people, places, and things that bring you joy.

What makes you stop and smile?

_____

Are there things that you do for others that will create a smile when a memory slips into their mind?

_____

Have you considered developing opportunities to create memories for yourself and others?

_____

What memory treasures can you give to others?

_____

ii. Schedule in a time to sit quietly and reflect on the following questions:

_____

Who do you interact with on a daily basis?

_____

How important is your relationship with these individuals?

_____

If asked, what would your family, friends, and colleagues say about your contributions to their lives?

_____

What would they say about your life achievements to date?

_____

What would they say about your character?

_____

REFERENCES

1. Gilliland, Steve. 2013. *Hide Your Goat.* Advantage Media Group.

2. Gilliland, Steve. 2004. *Enjoy the Ride.* Insight Pub. Co.

3. Ross, Gilbert, "7 Morning Rituals to Empower Your Day and Change Your Life," accessed July 1, 2015, "http://www.lifehack.org/articles/lifestyle/7-morning-rituals-empower-your-day-change-your-life.html.

4. Smith Jones, Susan. 2010. *The Joy Factor.* Red Wheel/Weiser

5. Ross, Gilbert, "7 Morning Rituals to Empower Your Day and Change Your Life"

6. Winfrey, Oprah. 2014. *What I Know For Sure.* Flatiron Books.

7. Siegel, Wendy Meg. 2012. *The Gratitude Habit: A 365 Day Journal and Workbook: A tool for creating positive feelings in your daily life.* CreateSpace Independent Publishing Platform.

8. *Rideau: Roy Saunderson's Blog,* accessed July 1, 2015. http://rideau.com/blogs/roy-saunderson.

9. *Jim Rohn,* accessed July 1, 2015. http://www.jimrohn.com.

10. Gilliland, Steve. *Enjoy the Ride.*

11. Gilliland, Steve. *Hide Your Goat.*

12. *Bryant McGill,* accessed July 1, 2015, http://bryantmcgill.com.

13. Jones, Susan Smith. 2010. *The Joy Factor.* Red Wheel/Weiser.

14. McGhee, Paul, "The Laughter Remedy," accessed July 1, 2015, http://www.laughterremedy.com.

15. "Laughter Therapy," accessed July 1, 2015, http://www.theguardian.com/lifeandstyle/2008/jul/06/healthandwellbeing4.

16. *Loma Linda University.* "LLU researcher finds that anticipating happy times may have health benefits," accessed July 1, 2015, http://www.llu.edu/news/today/today_story.page?id=1621.

17. Mandela, Nelson. 1995. *Long Walk to Freedom.* Little, Brown Book Group.

18. Williams, Pat. 2012. *Tom Osborne on Leadership: Life Lessons from a Three-Time National Championship Coach.* Advantage Media Group.

19. Welch, Jack, and Suzy Welch. 2007. *Winning.* HarpersCollins.

20. Drucker, Peter F. 2009. *The Essential Drucker: Management, the Individual and Society.* HarpersCollins.

21. Locke, Robert, "7 Ways to Tell the Difference Between Real Leadership and Good Management," accessed July 1, 2015, http://www.lifehack.org/articles/work/7-ways-tell-the-difference-between-real-leadership-and-good-management.html.

22. Goleman, Daniel, "What Makes a Leader," accessed July 1, 2015, https://hbr.org/2004/01/what-makes-a-leader.

23. Ovans, Andrea, "How Emotional Intelligence Became a Key Leadership Skill," accessed July 1, 2015, https://hbr.org/2015/04/how-emotional-intelligence-became-a-key-leadership-skill&cm_sp=Article-_-Links-_-Top%20of%20Page%20Recirculation.

24. Bokhari, Dean, "25 Books That Will Teach the Most Powerful Leadership Lessons," accessed July 1, 2015, http://www.lifehack.org/articles/productivity/25-books-that-will-teach-the-most-powerful-leadership-lessons.html.

25. *Goodreads,* accessed July 1, 2015, http://www.goodreads.com/quotes/tag/legacy.

26. Buffett, Warren, "My Philanthropic Pledge," accessed July 1, 2015, http://givingpledge.org/Content/media/My%20Philanthropic%20Pledge.pdf.

27. Osburn, Jan Johnston, "Time to Write a New Chapter in Your Life? Five Ways to Get You Started," accessed July 1, 2015, http://www.lifehack.org/articles/communication/time-write-new-chapter-your-life-five-ways-get-you-started.html.

Printed in the USA
CPSIA information can be obtained
at www.ICGtesting.com
JSHW012036140824
68134JS00033B/3092

9 781599 325972